50 SECRETS
How to Meet People and Make Friends

By
Chet Cunningham

UNITED RESEARCH PUBLISHERS

50 SECRETS
How to Meet People and Make Friends

First published in the United States of America in 1992 by United Research Publishers, P.O. Box 2344, Leucadia, California 92024.

Library of Congress Catalog Card Number 91-068345

ISBN 0-9614924-7-3

Printed in the United States of America
10 9 8 7 6 5 4 3 2 1

Dedicated to Rose Marie, my wife, who is my best friend and a friend to all who meet her. She meets and greets better than anyone I know. She's a good example of the *right way* to meet people and to make friends.

Order additional copies
of this book from:

UNITED RESEARCH PUBLISHERS
P.O. Box 2344
Leucadia, CA 92024

FULL 30-DAY MONEY-BACK GUARANTEE IF NOT SATISFIED

CONTENTS

INTRODUCTION

Everyone wants to be at ease meeting new people and to be able to make friends. We want to be liked and comfortable in all kinds of social situations. Too often many of us feel like Willy Loman did in Arthur Miller's classic play, DEATH OF A SALESMAN. Willy said: "Oh, I'm liked, I'm just not *well* liked."

We want to be well liked, we want to be able to meet new people without a trace of nervousness or a queasy stomach, we want to know how to be casual and friendly, know how to turn strangers into friends. In short how to unlock the "real you" and have people like you.

That's what this book is going to do for you. The title says fifty secrets to do all of this. Frankly there are probably three times that many, but I didn't want to scare anybody off.

Yes, there are little "tricks of the trade" in meeting and greeting people and learning to become at ease and casual in social situations. Many of them are common sense, ordinary, every day methods that you've probably thought of but just never got around to trying out in practice.

For example, you probably think the main way we communicate with others is by the spoken word. It's vital later on, but that's not the first way a new person makes that important original first impression of you. That almost always comes *visually*.

You walk into a room with a friend to a six person dinner party. No one there but your friend knows you, but she knows everyone else. There are four sets of eyes evaluating you that first moment you come in the door. They are absorbing facts about you, checking you over, speculating about you, some making up their minds about you before you ever open your mouth.

You come in the door *following* your date. A few points with the non feminists. You belch, scratch your chest and stumble over a chair falling flat on your face because you were staring at your hostess's cleavage.

There, we have a lot we know about this guy before he rips off a yard and a half of swear words.

Not only actions, but *body language* plays a big part in how you communicate. For example, if you stand with your arms folded across your chest and a frown on your face, or maybe one hand covering your mouth, you are giving the impression to everyone who looks at you that you don't want to talk to anyone. You're saying go away, leave me alone, I'm happy here being miserable and I don't need anybody trying to cheer me up, or brighten my day or talk about the local sports team.

This book will tell you a lot about body language, how it can help you to show others that you are ready, willing and eager to talk to them.

Maybe you're worried about how to approach someone and start talking to them. I'll give you a dozen or more helps you can use to start a conversation. The best way is to make the first move. Walk up to someone not deep in talk with someone else and say: "Hi, I'm Jane." Ninety times out of 89 the other person will smile and be thankful you came and give you his name and whammo, you're off on a conversation.

One of the best ways to get people to like you is for

you to remember *their names*. Names are so common, we all have them. But to every man and woman, their name, how it is spelled and pronounced, is one of the most important parts of their personality. Pronounce a person's name wrong, and most will jump right in, interrupt even the President of the United States and say that's Smythe, not Smith. It's almost a reflex with us.

For much the same reason, people like to hear their own names. Take advantage of that weakness by learning people's names when you meet them. This book gives half a dozen easy ways to memorize people's names.

Try this sometime. Meet someone new and remember the name. Then call that person by name three or four times that evening, and before it's over, that person will also call you by name. They will ask someone who you are and make it a point to let you know that they remember you, as well.

I'm going to spend a lot of time talking about how you can make friends. It's easier than you might think it is. What the book shows you are lots of ways for you to be open and friendly and honest and genuine so a normal friendship will have a chance to develop. When we're talking about making a new friend at a meeting or a dinner, or a social gathering, it usually starts with a "Hi, I'm Phil, what's your name?" A great smile and friendly body language goes along with the opening. It isn't a line, a con, or a seduction. It's a friendly approach to someone you don't know and decide that you'd like to take a flyer at meeting that person.

The same techniques can work equally well in business. Say you're at a business luncheon and you've been wanting to meet the top man in your field who is there. He won't bite. Walk up and introduce yourself, your company and throw in a gentle compliment about reading one of his articles, or hearing a speech. Part of it is making that first approach. Most of these really outstanding persons got there partly because they are good with people and will be genuinely warm and helpful with you. We'll have some helps for you along this line, too.

Some people never have friends over because they simply are afraid of trying to entertain. "I wouldn't know what to say," is a common complaint. In this book I go to your party, show you some easy clues about how to circulate, to introduce single people standing around looking bored, how to keep everyone having a good time.

I'll even give you some suggestions how to talk to an obnoxious guest and get rid of him before he ruins your party.

A lot of people these days simply don't know how to ask someone for a date or to give an invitation. A lot of what you've learned from the general meeting and greeting comes to play here but there are special tips as well.

Of course make it clear if it's to be a social gathering for drinks and talk, or a sit down dinner, or a night out for just the two of you. I'll show you how to approach a man, and how to approach a woman. Of course, one clue is to make the invitation perfectly clear and be sure it is a fun sounding evening or outing.

Even with all of our techniques for meeting people, some of you will still have anxiety about meeting strangers or going to a gathering where you know absolutely no one. I'll highlight the ideas of positive thinking and how they can result in positive action and help reduce that anxiety level to zero!No one there will kill you. Establish a strong self image and project it as you say hello to someone and get a conversation going. The biggest point here is to try it. Soon you'll find that talking to strangers at the supermarket or in line at the post office or while waiting for a bus will be easy and natural.

One of the toughest talking situations most of us ever find ourselves in is visiting friends who are ill, or are grieving after a death. What can you say? How do you do it? How can you help rather than make the person feel worse? I'll cover this in some detail, because what are friends for?

A friend of mine went to see a terminally ill man and before long the hospital room was filled with uproarious laughter.

The two old friends had decided to forget the future, forget the pain and the suffering. They had two hours of recalling their wild youth in the Marines, and some of the leaves they were on in San Diego and then in Honolulu. The afternoon rushed past and when visiting hours were over the ill man felt a hundred times better than before the visit. Whenever you can bring a happy afternoon to an ill person. This kind of friendship becomes some of the best medicine that a seriously ill or grieving person can get.

Sometimes we need to 'whoa back horse' and take a better look at our personal lives. Maybe it's time that we consider our own relationships. How are we communicating with our spouse? Is our marriage a "friendly" situation? What about man/woman communications and all of the current pop-psychology books that tell us women and men are so terribly different? Many books now are telling us that men and women are really much more alike than the detractors want us to believe.

I want to deal for a while in this book with the business world. Can a person make friends in business? Is it all cutthroat and rivalries and one-ups-manship? What about the good human values that work so well in a social situation? Can't they apply even to your boss and his boss and those people who also work under you?

For a time the book will be discussing how you can improve your self image. How much better to make friends with others, if you know for sure just who you are and what you stand for and how you can present yourself in the most realistic light.

To top off this whole book I'll close with a solid, never to be missed list of fifty secrets how you can meet people and make friends.

I was in New York City recently. Suddenly Madison avenue was flooded with what I assumed were four million people. The sidewalk was one mass of bouncing heads as I looked down a slight incline. Four blocks of jammed together bobbing heads and shoulders stretched from street to stores, all rapidly heading somewhere that each individual was intent upon reaching.

I settled back against a business window and watched. What a mass of humanity! How in the world could anyone ever communicate with any of those people?

Then I saw a woman with a cane coming across the street. Just as she got to the sidewalk, she hit her cane on the curb and stumbled. She caught herself but a package fell from her arms. She looked down at the package and shook her head. One man hit it with his foot as he passed. A second did a little jig to miss it. The third man, who was somewhere in his early sixties, stopped, picked up the package and handed it to the woman.

She thanked him.

He gave her one of the brightest smiles I've ever seen. He was dressed in a trim business suit, his tie straight, handkerchief in his jacket pocket, his hair meticulously combed. His eyes sparkled as he nodded accepting her thanks.

"Everyone seems to be in such a rush," the woman said.

"Not everyone," the man replied with a soft smile. "I figure that I've got thirty-two years yet, so why should I be in a rush?"

Not a bad idea. Take a little time for yourself. Go through this book and figure out what ideas you can use to spark up your own ability to say "Hi" and make friends. I think you'll agree that the time will be well spent.

The next time I see you, I hope you'll put on a big smile, uncross your arms and come forward and say, "Hi, I'm Mary Jones. How is the evening going with you?"Most of you probably have a lot more than 32 years left in your life span. So what's *your* hurry. Take a moment and dig into this book chapter by chapter and see if it can't make a difference in how you meet and greet people and how you make friends.

Where to start? Let's start right at the beginning. That moment when you step through a door and six people make that instantaneous and dreaded, *first impression.*

Try to read a chapter and make one little change in how you do something. Maybe you usually stand with your arms crossed. Now you know that's not the best way to do it. Consciously stand with your hands at your sides or even one in your pocket or behind you.

Then see what you can pick up from each chapter. Hey, you'll be surprised how all of these little tidbits will add up to a lot more interesting life.

Take a chance! Now, the best way to do this is to turn the page and dig right in and say Hi, to chapter one.

1

MEETING AND GREETING...
ANYONE

It was a Neighborhood Watch potluck, where everyone on our suburban block got together to meet the new people who had moved in, to trade jokes and banter and to let the petty crooks know that we were watching for them. Fred and Phyllis had moved in next door to me and I conned them into coming. Fred said he didn't like parties. I told him this was just the people on the block, maybe thirty or forty ordinary folks with kids and dogs and the whole thing in our back yard with picnic tables borrowed from neighbors.

Fred and Phyllis came. We even had name tags, a must for a situation like this. I got busy trying to find more chairs and benches just when Fred and Phyllis came so I couldn't take them around and introduce them to everyone. I knew I should have.

When I got the chairs located and back in the patio where the soft drinks and iced tea were, I saw Fred. He had pasted himself against a patio post. He wore a small frown and his arms were folded and one leg crossed over the other. Then he moved one hand and covered his mouth as if he were deep in thought.

He looked miserable. Fred was showing the worst possible impression to the rest of the people. He had the traditional

1

"body language" that says: Don't bother me. I don't want to be here and I'm not talking to anyone. His folded arms, his crossed legs, his frown and his hand over his mouth indicated to these friendly neighbors that here was a tough nut and he should be left alone.

I grabbed Fred and told him a joke on myself and got him to chuckle. Then I took him around and introduced him to the best looking ladies on our block. At once, Fred perked up. I had lost his wife Phyllis.

Fred started to relax. He even told a joke. Before long Fred found another man who was a nut about model railroads, had his whole two car garage given over to a set built up waist high with four different trains and enough buildings and landscaping to keep him busy for years. They talked trains the rest of the night.

At first, Fred had showed the worst possible signals to anyone around him. They were "stay away" signs and everyone could read them easily. Remember, others are as shy and uncomfortable as you are about meeting new people. If they see the "don't bother me" signals, they aren't going to take a chance on being the first to say hello.

THE OPEN POSTURE

So here's your how to meet people hint number one: Stand and sit with an "open" posture. Keep your hands off your face especially don't cover your mouth. Keep your arms uncrossed, casually at your side or if sitting, put them in your lap. Make sure that you don't have your legs crossed.

To reinforce this open posture, put on a big smile. You don't have to have a smile pasted on all the time and look like an idiot child just out of the home. However if someone looks at you, smile at them, send out the signal to them that you are friendly and open to meet them and talk.

A lot of us tend to stand with our arms crossed, more men than women do this, not from any anger or impatience, just pure habit.

So reverse the habit, stand with one hand in your pocket if you have to or behind your back, to remind yourself not to cross your arms.

Psychologists tell us that crossed arms can imply that you are in a defensive frame of mind and combative, not ready to talk to anyone. Crossed arms can also make others feel that you are impatient, that you're showing displeasure, or that you are framing a judgement and telling the whole world to stay away.

A lot of people do stand with arms crossed, but often this is pure habit. The next time you have to stand for a while, without moving, check your posture. Are your arms folded? Is most of your weight on one foot and the other one crossed at the ankle? Are you frowning?

By using an open posture and a smile, you'll charge through the biggest drawback of bad body language and be ready to surge ahead into this meeting and greeting social situation.

TRY YOUR SMILE

With the Open Posture mentioned above, we add a smile. There is nothing that welcomes a stranger more than a smile. There is nothing that shows people who don't know you that you want to be friendly more than a smile. Besides that, there is nothing that makes a pretty woman or a handsome man, *more attractive* than a great smile.

Most pictures of models selling jewelry or clothes or other high ticket items show these beautiful women who aren't smiling. Why? Some say because the smile would overpower the product. The product is what's being sold here not the model or her or his smile. They have a point.

If someone looks at you 'across a crowded room' and smiles, you get the distinct impression that the person is looking upon you with some kind of favor, and would not object to a smile in return and perhaps even a bit of conversation. You should do the same thing.

When you meet someone, try out your best smile, just for starters. Chances are the other person will think: "Hey, here is a guy or a girl who isn't going to rip my face off and throw it at me. Why don't I smile back and say Hi, and maybe even talk a while?"

Then there is the fact that it is easier to smile than to frown. Somebody proved that it takes more facial muscles and more energy expended to frown than it does to smile. So just to conserve your energy for more important things, you should smile more.

Let's say you're going into a meeting or a social affair where you know no one. That won't last long. First smile at everyone, sit or stand in your open manner that will show you're friendly and ready to communicate with someone. Chances are that you won't be sitting by yourself for long.

ALWAYS SIT TALL

In the old West, the hero always 'sat tall in the saddle'. He was sitting erect, leaning forward just a little, ready for any kind of action.

The same thing works today in the hard riding cocktail and party circuit. By sitting erect and leaning slightly forward when you're talking to someone, you give them the impression that you are interested in what they're saying, that you are listening intently to their words, and that perhaps you are interested in them as a person.

If you're talking to someone and he leans back and closes

4

his eyes, laces his fingers behind his head or stares at the ceiling, you could have the idea that the person is bored to tears with you and what you're saying, but he's too exhausted to move to where he can catch a small nap.

In China for years a person of lower rank would always sit on the side of the chair and then use only about one quarter of the available sitting space. This was a sign of respect for the more important person being consulted. Talk about sitting straight and tall! There was no room in that situation to be sloppy or to lean back and if you don't lean slightly forward you'll fall off the chair. Think of our Chinese friends when you sit down and start talking to someone. You don't have to sit on the front two inches of the chair, but sit tall and don't get too comfortable.

Always remember to sit tall in the saddle, pardner, but be sure your spurs don't snag on that expensive oriental rug.

SHAKE HANDS

In some parts of our country and in some levels of society, the "hello kiss" and the "hello hug" are routine. For most of us, however, the most acceptable form of first touching a friend or a stranger, is the hand shake.

Generally today the hand shake is used in social situations, in business, even in sports when you lose. Today a woman is often the first to offer to shake hands, and no one is surprised or upset by this small social change.

Almost anytime one person offers to shake hands, the other person will comply and shake. To ignore a handshake or refuse to shake hands is usually reserved for situations of extreme stress or long standing feuds or hatreds. We're not worried about those.

Just as women can offer to shake hands first, so the man

5

can offer to shake hands with a woman.

The natural thing to do when shaking hands is to introduce yourself: "Hi, I'm President Adams. It's nice to meet you." This will almost always get the other person to respond and give their name.

Shaking hands is a friendly greeting, a way physically to touch the other person in an accepted manner and shows a warmth and is non-aggressive.

In some countries a man will kiss a woman's hand on greeting, but it's a surprise now when it happens here unless the man is from a society where that is common.

What about the hug-hug bunch? This is a social strata type of thing. I've seen some churches where it is common practice for everyone to hug everyone else. These were not polite shoulder to shoulder hug, but full body hugs.

This becomes a situational concern. If everyone in the group hugs friends, then go along if it doesn't make you feel uncomfortable.

In a new situation watch and see what the others do. Most people in polite society do not use the "hug everybody" approach. To some people this is an intrusion on their "space" and their privacy.

On the other hand if you have friends whom you genuinely like and enjoy and have known for some time and they don't object, then by all means use this form of touching and hug away.

TO KISS OR NOT TO KISS:

The kiss greeting is common in the Hollywood scene, but even there it is not a universal.

I've known a lot of actors and they seem to have a kiss and hug behavior going strong. Even college students in the acting and drama field developed this kiss on greeting syndrome. Perhaps it was genuine, perhaps it was to set them apart from the others in the school, but it was common through the whole department.

Kissing on greeting is quite common in many foreign countries, all over Europe and Latin America especially. It is common for men to kiss men and women to kiss women on the cheeks with no concern. Small children are taught to kiss their relatives and the custom continues.

Whether you want to kiss your close friends on greeting is partly cultural, partly situational but mostly personal. If you have a true affection for someone of long standing, the cheek kiss can be a powerful way to show your feelings in a polite and accepted way.

EYE CONTACT

If you're walking down the street in a big town, most people are careful to avoid eye contact with strangers. It can send the wrong signal and can cause all sorts of trouble.

However, in a social or business situation, eye to eye contact when being introduced to someone or when talking with a person, is a dramatic and important way to show that person that you're listening, that you're interested, and that you're pleased to be there.

When you combine the other elements listed above, including that great smile, with eye contact, you're showing whoever you may be talking to that you're interested and pleased and that what they are saying is important.

Don't stare at a person. Eye to eye contact should be broken now and then, then re-established. You might move your focus around the person's face, then back to his or her eyes. You might look across the room, then come back and look at the person's eyes and concentrate there for a moment.

7

Staring or leering at a person can give the wrong idea and may make the other person suspicious of your intentions. If the other person is also watching you during these times, it will give you more confidence as well.

I had a friend in college who was a psychology major and he was full of eye contact studies. One night at a dance, he never looked at the girl's eyes, he always stared at the top of her head. Every girl he asked to dance made it a point to dance only once with him. None would accept a second dance.

The next dance we went to he used polite normal eye contact and even though he was not a great dancer, he had no trouble finding partners, or dancing two or three sets with the same one.

So remember eye contact. It gives the person you're talking to the idea that here is an alive, real human being who appreciates what I'm saying and thinks that I'm interesting.

PUT IT ALL TOGETHER:

Now, remember that whole books have been written on body language. Enough for now to know that if you use these five body language tips, you'll be well on your way to meeting someone and starting an interesting conversation.

Remember always to use AN OPEN POSTURE, to be sure to SMILE and SAY HELLO. Offer to SHAKE HANDS and give your name. When you sit down be sure to SIT STRAIGHT and lean forward when you talk. Always make sure to establish EYE CONTACT with whoever you're talking to.

RISK SAYING HELLO FIRST

Well, how does this "new you" feel so far? Here you are at your first social event after reading the book. You're all set with an OPEN POSTURE, you've been smiling your face off and now over your glass you see a guy looking at you who is at least half a hunk and he's smiling.

But will he come over and say hi?

Now is the time to throw out all those old wive's tales about "how a lady should act" and walk up and RISK SAYING HELLO FIRST. It's a deliciously small risk. Give it a try. So you do. He sees you coming and looks away, then looks back when you plant your size five's directly in front of him.

"Hi, I'm Emma Fitzgerald. How are you doing?"

You leave it hanging there and push out your hand. His eyes go wide and he gulps and takes your small hand in his big one and shakes politely. You're maintaining EYE CONTACT all this time and in a flash, he grins. It's a great grin.

"Hi, I'm Bert Charles. Things are looking up. Can I get you a drink? Oh, you already have one."

You're dazzling him with your best smile. "Yes, thanks. But I would like another one of those little finger sandwiches. Did you try them? I wonder what's in them?"

Zap! Bam! Schazam! You're off and running. By being the first one to say hello, you solve a lot of problems. You keep yourself out and moving around, you find half a dozen people to introduce yourself to and become acquainted with, just maybe one of them is an honest to goodness candidate for a real friend, and you solidify your own self image. Hey, you can do this "Hi I'm Emma" bit and smile and have an open posture and eye contact and it really isn't all that hard.

A couple of small notes about taking that risk. You say you've never done that in your life. How can you get up the nerve to just walk up to a stranger and start talking?

That means you've been a shy person all of your life. You've gone to parties and sat on the sidelines with a cup of punch and waited for someone to come and talk. Usually you sit and wait and wait and wait.

Yes, there is some danger of being rejected when you make the first move, but you temper the odds by walking around and watching for people with open postures, who are smiling, who look like they are interesting and one of them who returns your smile.

This isn't a seductive come on, it's just a simple, social contact. You as a modern woman can surely do that. You're not trying to pick him up in a singles bar. This is class, honest people, ordinary people just like you who are a little scared, too. So don't sit on the sidelines any longer being a conversationalist wallflower, get out there and take that small risk, and you'll have something to tell the girls, or the guys, tomorrow.

So, now, what's next?

ASKING THE RIGHT QUESTIONS

You've probably seen interviews on late night TV shows or daytime shows where the interviewer asks a question and the celebrity or subject of the day replies with one word answers.

This is usually what happens at first in our boy meets girl scenario. They are getting to know you questions.

"So, Bert, what work do you do?"

"I'm in microchips"

"Oh, here in town?"

"Out in little Silicone Valley."

"You must own your own company."

"Yes, but it's a small one."

But now we have some basis to go on so the next step is to ask the OPEN ENDED QUESTION. This is one that can't be answered in one or two words, it takes more time and more thought and leads to more involvement. Like this:

"Bert, how did you get into making microchips, anyway?"

Now, Bert has a chance to give her his life history if he wants to. It might take him five minutes to explain just how he wound up with his multi-million-dollar-in-sales firm.

The open ended question usually uses key words such as *how, why, in what way*.

In the first ritual "getting to know you" questions, Bert might have found out that Emma was a former ballet dancer who gave it up because there were no good jobs in town and she didn't want to go to San Francisco or Seattle. He finds out she's opened her own ballet dance studio and has four branches and twelve instructors working for her.

Now Bert might ask her a question like this:

"Emma, how did you go from a starving ballet dancer to owner of your first ballet dance studio?"

Now, Emma has a shot at doing some talking, giving information about herself and her background and her drive that made her into a business success. Most people enjoy talking about themselves. Who better to tell about yourself than someone who doesn't know you. Some of us have a tendency to gild the lily a little and put ourselves in the best possible light. But in between, there is a lot of solid, basic information about ourselves and our lives.

A psychologist said that many times people talking with someone for the first time will tell a stranger things about themselves that they never have told their spouse, or any of their good friends. It's a way we can spread out and just talk, and in the process we may be creating a new friend who could become highly important to us.

11

GUIDE THE CONVERSATION:

When you do most of the question asking, you can be the one to guide the conversation. If it veers into areas you don't want to talk about, such as sickness and deaths in the other person's family, you can steer it away from those.

"Bert, you said you used to play minor league baseball. What position did you play and how did you ever get involved in professional baseball?"

I know an extra who works in TV shows and movies. He told me it's mostly standing around for five or six hours and then having a fast five minutes of action in front of the cameras and then sitting around again as the technicians set up the next shot and fix the lights and test it all. He said once he was teamed with an attractive lady in a lunch situation where they overlooked the pool where the stars were in action.

They sat there for four hours.

As they both had learned, the best way to pass the time is to talk, and they did. Before the director yelled "That's a wrap for today, people," my buddy and his new friend knew a tremendous lot about each other. Both were married and had children and in the hours of talking they became good friends and looked for each other when the calls came for the next movie or TV show to be shot in San Diego.

KNOW WHEN TO CUT AND RUN:

One basic to remember. If you have been talking with someone for a half hour and you find nothing of mutual interest and you've decided you want to move on to another person, don't stay there and keep asking questions. Soon the other person will realize you're not being sincere in your interest and it will make that person uncomfortable.

Simply stand and shake hands with the person, wish him luck in his work and say you need to get across the room to talk to an old friend.

There are a few easy ways to make mistakes when first meeting someone. One of the most common is to say: "Hello, How are you?" Why a mistake? It's a sterile, insincere rote question. You really don't want to know the aches and pains and pills and doctors with which this person is involved. It's an insincere question. It usually gets an equally insincere answer: "Oh, I'm fine, how are you?"

Another danger zone is to get too personal with people you know, but haven't seen for a while: "Well John, you got away from the old ball and chain for the night. How is the old lady?" John might lift his brows, frown and say: "I think she's at peace. My Jane died over a year ago."

With a person you've just met, be careful about getting too personal as well. Keep the questions general and on the lighter side. Most of the time stay away from the two problem question areas of religion and politics. Both of them can kill you.

Be careful not to ask open ended questions which are so broad that no one can answer them. These might include: "What can we do about the ecology problem? How can we get the American people to take part in the political life of the nation? What in the world can we do to stop drive by shootings?"

Try not to ask leading questions. They will only result in a yes or no answer and the ball is back in your court.

LISTEN TO THE OTHER PERSON:

Often you can figure out what questions to ask someone you've just met by listening to what he or she is saying.

Emma might hear Bert talking about a new smaller sized chip they are working on. She might key off this.

"Bert, how in the world did you ever figure out how to make those computer chips so tiny?"

Later he might talk about the competition from Japan but he says he's developed a chip that can't be copied and it will be used on the latest IBM computers. They will have to order all of those chips directly from Bert's company.

Emma might ask: "How in the world do you get a tie-in with a big computer manufacturing firm like that so you have an exclusive contract?"

Lots of times if you can't think of any questions to ask a person you've just met, it's because you haven't been listening to what the person was saying. Don't think of questions now, listen instead and the questions will come later.

Meeting people in a social or business situation doesn't have to be difficult. Relax, be more open, remember what a positive effect you can have on your social life and your business life.

BRING YOUR OWN PR PERSON:

One of the best ways to get a great introduction in a party or a business affair is to bring along your own public relations person. Someone who will introduce you to people. This would be a friend who might say:

"Bert, I want you to meet Emma Fitzgerald. Emma has been our top producing time salesman for the past six months and looks like she's on her way to becoming our sales manager. What do you think of that and she's only been with our firm for two years."

How could a person pass up an introduction like that. I've seen people who go to events and plan on introducing each other at various times to different people this way. It sets up a world of confidence for the one being introduced, and gets conversation off to a fast start.

Now you have met someone, maybe talked a little. What are some sure fire ways to start a good conversation with that person? Some have been hinted at above, but in the next chapter we'll take a more detailed look at them.

2

STARTING A CONVERSATION

So far, so good. You've picked up some new ideas in the previous chapter about how to meet people, how to be open and smile and all the rest. We even talked a little about how to get started talking to someone. That was just the warm up. Now we go into the graduate level in conversation starting.

1. FIND THE RIGHT PERSON

The best rule in starting a conversation is to find someone else who is interested in talking, looking forward to meeting someone new, or trying to find someone to talk to.

Look for the person with all of the openness qualities we talked about in chapter one. Someone with an open stance, who can smile, who is ready to look you in the eye and give you a good firm handshake.

At a party, program or meeting, most people are pleased to be able to meet someone new and have a good conversation with them. If a person is not in the middle of a chat with half a dozen other people, and smiles when you do and doesn't run away as you approach, you probably have found a good prospect.

Members of the other sex may let you know of their interest in several other ways. They may look back at you several times, may adjust their clothes, rub their hands or perhaps smooth the arm of a chair.

Take the direct approach. Make the first move yourself. Move toward the person, make eye contact, smile, hold out your hand and introduce yourself.

"Hi, I'm Bill Zollinger. I was hoping I'd get through the crowd before you vanished somewhere."

She laughed. "I'm Wanda Ettinger, and I'm not in the habit of vanishing."

"It seems like most of the people here are bankers or are in the motion picture business. *The business*, as we call it."

"That's why I'm here. I'm a writer and I have a script or two I'm shopping around."

"How interesting. I wish I was a producer looking for a script. I'm a film director."

What a great start. You both are in the same field, you're pleasant and have started talking, learning about each other. You're off and running.

2. THAT OPENING LINE

No, don't worry about finding exactly the right "line" to use in an opening. Just don't go with the old stale and trite ones.

- "At last I've found the most beautiful girl in the room."
- "They never told me there would be so many handsome men here."
- "I know that I've met you before, I can't remember where."
- "I've been past here three times tonight, how could I have missed meeting you?"

17

Almost anything you say after Hi, is going to help break the ice. Of course don't use a negative opening. Don't say something like: "Wow, it's so hot in here I don't know why I stay." The other person may agree with you and suggest: "If it's too hot for you, why don't you leave." With that she might turn and walk away.

The important thing is to say SOMETHING. Be the first to break the ice, to make the approach, and you're halfway there. Why? Because while you may have a few butterflies in the old gut, the other person might be so nervous and on edge that he or she is about ready to throw up. Nerves can do funny things to people.

One of the best ways to open a conversation with a stranger is a compliment. "What a pretty sweater you're wearing. Did you get it here in town or from Europe?" You pay a compliment and ask a question. Most people react well to compliments. It makes them feel good and they almost always respond.

Other easy opening subjects are the party hostess, the food at the party, or even asking the time. At a bus stop you could ask someone when the bus will come. In line at the supermarket you might ask the person behind you about some product in your grocery cart.

Right after that first line and her response, try asking a question. It can be simple and direct.

"So, Wanda. What kind of scripts do you write? Historicals, thrillers or romances?"

It's an easy to answer question, it could even have a one word answer, but it gets things moving

Let's stop here and talk a minute about the fear of being rejected or ignored. What happens if the person you've approached looks surprised you're there, gives you a frown and turns around and walks away?

You pull back your hand and keep walking and looking for someone else who might be interested in talking. Think of it as though you're playing baseball. You're still at the plate until that third strike, and even then it might be a foul ball and you're still alive.

If one person rejects your offer of a friendly talk, it isn't the end of the world. We all get rejected at times. Writers and actors get rejected more than anyone else. They learn to live with it.

Take an actor going on a casting call or a commercial. His agent has sent in his picture and a director has told his agent to send in Jones at 2:30 on Tuesday for an audition. The part is for a contemporary businessman so a coat and tie would be appropriate.

Bill shows up on time, signs in and waits his turn. There in the room and spilling outside are 35 men all about the same age, all wearing suits and ties and hair combed in the businessman's fashion.

Right away Bill knows he's a 35 to one shot to get the part. Then he hears that they have been auditioning this way for four days. They have already looked at over 200 men and may look at another 200. That makes the odds 400 to one.

Bill gets his turn with the director who has him give his name and agent to the video camera, turn right, turn left. The director asks Bill to read the "sides" or the lines on a Xeroxed sheet of paper.

Bill reads them. The director says give it a little more emphasis, he's in a sad, almost tearful mood. Bill does it again, and the director says thanks. We'll be in touch with you.

Bill goes out and heads for his next audition for a small part in an industrial training movie. Bill won't even think about the audition again. If he gets a call back, fine. If not he keeps going to auditions until he lands a part. What he doesn't do is dwell on how he probably won't get the part, not at 400 to one.

19

An actor might be rejected 150 or 200 times at in person interviews before he is selected for the part in a commercial or a play or a movie. They learn how to cope with rejection.

Anyone can do the same. The secret is to forget about it. don't dwell on the past. Think about the next audition, the next person you want to walk up to and say hello and start talking.

It's not that hard.

3. ASK THOSE RITUAL QUESTIONS

Bill and Wanda had started to ask each other questions. That's the best way to begin. It's like a blank piece of paper. You know nothing about each other, so you ask simple and direct questions to get some basis for more talking.

"You asked me what kind of scripts I write," Wanda said. "Actually I'm on a binge of doing thrillers, with wild maniacal killers. What kind of movies do you direct?"

"Lately I've been doing specials for television. Do you live around here?"

"Out in the valley. But I don't have to drive in every day. Where do you live?"

"In the Hollywood Hills. An apartment. Have you had any of your scripts produced?"

Now, the few simple questions have created a lot in common for Bill and Wanda. They both are "in the business". Wanda writes scripts and Bill directs. She lives in the valley and he lives in the Hollywood Hills. They are moving along nicely. They are smiling and chatting like old friends. Only they aren't yet.

4. MOVE ON TO OPEN END QUESTIONS

Now is the time to dig a little deeper, to move on to the open ended questions so you can learn a little more about the person. Wanda might say:

"I've always wondered just how a director goes about getting a job to direct a picture."

"No secret. I belong to the Director's Guild, and most directors depend on their reputation and their list of credits to get them new jobs. Of course gatherings like this don't hurt any. So far I've talked to three producers and reminded them that I'm going to be free in two months for a new assignment."

Away they go, as Bill talks about his profession, which is a vital interest to Wanda.

Soon Bill might have a question:

"Wanda, how in the world do you writers come up with the wild crazy terror filled ideas for those suspense scripts?"

As the conversation moves along, the couple might visit the bar for fresh drinks, or the snack table, or find some chairs and sit and talk.

This exchange of facts about each other is what psychologists call giving "free information". The longer two people talk, the more they learn about each other. Everytime you answer a question by someone, you are providing a wealth of data and facts about yourself, your background, your vocation and soon your hopes and fears as well.

That's what conversation is all about. It's the best and quickest way to get to know somebody. Journalists have found this out quickly. They might research a famous person for a week. Read everything they can about the person. Then they have a face to face talk with the star or politician or sports figure, and many times they must do a fast turn around about their pre-formed impressions of the individual.

21

The in-person conversation usually reveals a lot about a person that might not be learned in any other way.

These questions you ask and answer, quickly let you know if this is someone you would like to get to know better. Should you ask him or her out for dinner in a public place? You could meet there so each would be free to leave if necessary.

The use of questions can help you lead the conversation in the direction you want it to go. If it's about work and you want to talk about how to find the best vacation spot, a question is the way to shift the tone of the talk off business and to the South Seas or Hawaii or the Poconos.

5. HOW TO REMEMBER THOSE NEW NAMES

Let's say that Bill and Wanda have been talking for an hour by now. They find they know a few of the same people, enjoy some of the same cafes, and Wanda sees a friend who stops by to say hello.

Wanda is about to introduce her new friend to her old friend when Bill's name just vanishes right out of her memory. What can she do?

First, don't panic. In a case like this the easiest thing to do is to turn to Bill and say:

"I'm sorry, but I've been having such a good time talking to you, I've completely forgotten your name."

"Bill Zollinger."

"Bill right, you do know your name. I'm glad you didn't forget."

Wanda can make a little joke on herself, than go ahead and introduce Bill to her friend, and the social process goes on.

There are ways to help you remember names. Many times I have avoided someone at a party because for the life of me I can't remember the person's name, and I should because I've known the man and his wife for ten years. How can I cover up not knowing his name?

First, there's hope even for us. There are ways to help us remember names and we're going to go into them in detail.

Names are important to everyone. When you remember a person's name you just met an hour ago, or an old friend you haven't seen for ten years, it makes that person feel special. They are sure that you appreciate them and respect them.

Of course if you forget the person's name the exact opposite reaction is all too common. How to bridge the name remembering gap?

Let's take the person you are just meeting. How can you remember that person's name?

Most of us are a bit nervous when we meet somebody for the first time. We want to make a good impression and we might fiddle with our tie or our blouse or skirt. What this does is take our mind off what's going on.

Don't think about what you're going to say to this person, not right then. You need to do three things when you're introduced.

• Clear your mind of everything but the person's name. Listen carefully and hear it correctly.

• Now, repeat the name to yourself three or four times, silently, Joe Johnson, Joe Johnson, Joe Johnson.

• Next, use the person's name in conversation. "Well, Joe Johnson, it's good to meet you. I've seen your art work in the local gallery. I love your oils."

If you do these three things, you'll have a much better chance of remembering a person's name. As the conversation goes along, repeat the person's name again. "Joe Johnson. We had some neighbors named Johnson who live near us. Would the Charles Johnson's be any relation?"

Now, maybe something happens that you didn't hear the name during the introduction. It might be a blast of music from somewhere or a raucous thunder of laughter. Take the honest approach.

Say, "I'm sorry but I didn't hear your name over the noise. What was your name again?" When he tells you again, make certain you hear it and then do the three things you need to do repeating it to yourself, and using it in conversation with the new friend.

You've already been doing the other things, you smiled, you introduced yourself, you have an open posture and you make good eye contact. So you've taken another step forward to become a more interesting, more confident, better social animal.... you.

What about long term memory of a person's name? This gets a bit more complicated, but it's certainly something you can get working on as soon as you meet someone new.

Most memory experts have complicated thought association plans to help you remember names. One man says you should "take a mental photograph" of the person. This would be making careful note of the person's face the way an artist would. Oval face, mid ear sideburns, dark hair full and wavy, high cheekbones, heavy beard that shows a little even after a close shave, solid jaw and dark brown eyes that seem kind.

You put that description against the picture and file it away in those loops within loops in your brain's memory circuit with the tag line of Joe Johnson on it.

If you can equate the person's name with some emotional tag, that also will help you remember it. Say one of your favorite aunts name was Josephine. She died just two weeks ago. You can remember her and also this Joe as a person who was loosely linked with the death of your favorite aunt.

I have a friend who is a reporter and he's always taking notes, so it's not unusual for him to whip out his small pocket spiral notebook and write down something. Once I watched him and he wrote down the name of everyone he met at a party, and had a thumbnail sketch of each one.

With his reporter's mind he could go back through his notebook and give you an accurate police-report kind of description for fifteen or twenty people at that party.

If you're starting a new job with a new firm or department, it's a good plan to try the notebook idea. It works. When you meet new people, make a quick note of their name and department and their job. That night after work go over the list and repeat the names and their jobs. You'll be surprised how quickly you'll be remembering everyone you meet that way.

Pure association is what many experts suggest, but I keep running out of associations. Say Joe Johnson is a red head. How can that help you remember his name? Maybe you have a brother who is a red head and his name is Jack. So J equals red head, equals Joe Johnson, another red head. Might work.

The idea is that the next time you see this person you'll see that he's a red head and that will trigger your association with your brother the red head who is Jack. J then reminds you of Joe Johnson and you have his name.

This takes a lot of work on your part, and practice, and you sometimes have to come up with far fetched associations. But give it a whirl. It might be just the thing for you.

Let's see: Patty Orbach. Patty is heavy, five feet three. Your first unflattering association: Patty is a Fatty. Hey, if it works for you, try it. Of course never hint to anyone what your association word is for them. It will probably turn out that a lot of them will be uncomplimentary.

25

INTRODUCING YOURSELF

What if someone you just met forgets your name? You'll know it when you come up to them. A certified panic will steal over their face and they might stare wide eyed a minute. Cut through the panic and say:

"Hi, I'm Rebecca Sylvester, we met about a half hour ago and you were telling us how you caught that big marlin off the Kona coast in Hawaii."

This relives the pressure on others who might have forgotten your name — but you'll be assured that the next time they see you they will remember you.

I have one friend who is the smoothest at meeting and talking with strangers of anyone I've seen. She is slim, pert, pretty, bright eyed and always at the top of a bounce. I've never seen her sad or down. When she's in a group where people don't know her she comes up with a big smile and holds out her hand.

"Hi, I'm Chris Larabee. I work at Fletcher Inc. I love horses, hate football, spend half my salary on clothes and the rest buying golden oldie records of the forties and fifties."

What's not to like about Chris? She hits a favorite topic of at least half the people who hear her and the others hang around to see what interesting thing she's going to say next. Don't be afraid to give a little interesting capsule of yourself when you meet strangers.

STARTING A CONVERSATION

Keep to the basics. Ask the questions that you know will bring a response. Dig into the newcomer's answers and find subjects to use for more questions about the person. Look for free information about the person, and at the same time give him or her plenty of free information about yourself to keep the exchange going.

Eye contact is important at this point and all the way through a conversation. Concentrate on hearing correctly and remembering the individual's name as you're introduced. Use the name as you talk to help you remember it. The other person's name is important to him or her. Use it correctly and remember it. You'll be making points all the way.

Have you ever thought about using a conversation starter? This might be anything. One of the best is a book. Any controversial book is an excellent conversation starter. A book came out about how to commit suicide. It was a big best seller and was so controversial some stores wouldn't carry it.

Just holding it on your lap on a subway or bus, will usually bring a comment by someone close by.

"Oh, the suicide book," one older man said. "What did you think of it?"

An older woman the next day said: "You should be ashamed of yourself reading a book like that. Suicide is a sin, everyone knows that."

Any item that might get a response and lead to a conversation is a good one. I've always wanted to dummy up a book that was titled: MAKE YOUR OWN ATOMIC BOMB. I bet that would catch the eye of almost everyone within hailing distance.

Now we have our conversation well started. Some say getting moving is easy, how do you sustain it long enough to know if this is a person you would be comfortable with, or whom you might like to get to know better? How? Hey, we're here to help you do just that. So turn the page and read the next chapter.

3

KEEPING YOUR CONVERSATION GOING

So far, you've heard a lot of suggestions about how to meet and greet people, how to start a conversation, how to remember names and how to overcome those small rejections.

Now let's look at the highly important matter of keeping that fragile conversation going that you have established. We've talked about using free information you get and about the open ended question. Now we're going to move beyond that and get into some of the more detailed methods you can use to keep your talk going with this person in whom you're interested.

I. BE AWARE OF YOUR FACIAL AND BODY LANGUAGE:

Be continually aware of your own facial language and your body language as you continue to talk. Keep up the eye contact and the open posture. Make it easy for the other person to keep talking to you.

Be aware of the other person's *space*. Don't move in too close, but don't hold back too far away either. Soon this kind of facial and body language will become second nature and you'll be smiling at the right time, nodding to show that you're listening and concentrating on what the person is saying, really listening, so you can make relative comments.

Many of the experts say this is a good time for you to start asking personal questions. This means that you're going to have to be watchful and sensitive to the feelings of the other individual. If you can ask personal questions, it helps to bring the two of you closer and to extend the conversation and helps to lead to a new level of friendship.

Often you can precede the personal question with some kind of a disclaimer such as: "If you wouldn't mind telling me, I'd love to know...." Or, "If you don't mind me asking...." Or, "Just tell me if I'm being too personal, but...." Or, "Pardon me for being personal, but I'd really like to find out..."

This is a friendly, casual way of asking, yet lets the other individual have a clear option of not answering you. On the other hand, if you can get a breakthrough like this into more intimate aspects, it gives a real surge of friendliness to the conversation and lifts it to a new level.

If someone asks you a too-personal question, simply say you'd rather not talk about that right now and move on to another subject without letting time for the rejection to become overly important.

Sometimes people not only don't want to discuss personal information about themselves, they don't even want to tell you their name, where they live, what they do or who they know. If this happens, it makes the conversation a lot tougher, and knowing what the person doesn't want to talk about helps, but it might be just the time to cut and run with one of your good get away lines that we'll talk about later.

One of these is: "Oh, pardon me, but there is a friend of mine who was looking for me. I better find out what she wanted."

2. UTILIZE YOUR IMMEDIATE SURROUNDINGS:

Often keeping a conversation going is as simple as talking about where you are, a home, a meeting room, a ballroom, a fancy hotel, even a golf course or tennis court.

You can talk with the other person about the room or home itself, comment on the decor, ask what the other person knows about the place. Does it have any historic significance? Who is the host or hostess? What kind of a meeting is it? How long has this person been in the organization?

If it's a purely social situation you might ask the person where they first met the hostess, how their work ties in with the woman having the party.

By putting your focus on those around you, the indiviuals and the events taking place, you'll find dozens of things to talk about with a new friend. This is what is called looking "outward", rather than thinking about yourself. Now is not the time to worry if you wore the right dress or shoes, or if you combed your hair or shaved closely enough.

Relax and don't think about yourself, rather concentrate on the person you're talking with, and picking up hints and helps from him or her, and see what you can use from the surrounding area to help move your conversation along.

There's a new fire baton twirler and hula dance at this hotel's nightclub. Has the one you're talking to seen it? Has he ever been to Hawaii? What did he enjoy most in the Islands? Which one is his favorite? Has he visited all of them? Now you might tell about your trip off the Kona Coast when you went marlin fishing, and saw hundreds of porpoise.

Conversations lead down crooked roads. There is a fork every which way and one trail leads to another and the number of interesting subjects keeps growing. It's a wonderful indoor sport and in the process you can learn a great deal.

Let's say you've just met a new woman and she comments on a one-sheet motion picture poster of *Gone With The Wind* that is framed and hanging on the wall.

"Oh, *Gone With The Wind*, that's one of my favorite movies," Gwen said.

"I love that film," Phil said. "I've seen it twice now on TV. Is it out in video cassette yet, or are they saving it for another release?"

"I heard it's coming out on tape but I'm not sure when," Gwen said. "Are you a movie buff?"

"I try to see all of the five films nominated as the best of the year for the Oscars," Phil said.

"How do you know which ones will be nominated?"

"That's part of the fun," Phil said smiling. "You try to pick out the best ones as they are released, then when the nominations come out you get to go see the ones you missed."

"Hey a real movie fan," Gwen said. "I didn't think there were many of us left. Do you see the art films?"

"Art films! Just my favorites. I like the ones they put English subtitles on. But I get confused when the character on the screen says three sentences and the English translation is: 'Will you come with me.'"

They both laughed and hit it off. They talked during the rest of the party and made a date to go see a Fellini film the next night.

3. DON'T SPREAD RUMORS:

It's easy to keep talking to anyone by spreading rumors, or even starting them, or gossiping. This kind of small talk is always self defeating, and often will turn-off the person you're talking to. Play it safe and come up with some other topic to discuss.

Also you run the risk that this new individual you're

talking to is a friend of or even related to the person you're spreading the gossip about. That will get you a quick shut down in the conversation and the hasty exit by the person you were talking to.

4. WATCH FOR SPECIAL INTERESTS:

Look for special interests or pet projects of the person to whom you are talking. This is the absolutely best way to get a conversation going. If you find a subject that a man is especially interested in, he might talk your arm off before you can get him stopped.

This is great. Then you don't have to worry about keeping the conversation going. The other person does. If it happens to be a subject that interests you as well, such as the mating rituals of the fruit fly, which has only a four hour lifespan and must learn to do everything quickly, you're in luck.

These special interests might be the individual's work, hobby, a favorite charity, the theatre, sports, bungee cord jumping, cross training, pre-Colombian art. Whatever it is, and whether you know anything about it or not, it's a conversation extender.

All you need to do is say:

"Pre-Colombian art? I've never known much about it. Could you tell me something about it? Why are you so interested?"

With this small opening, the real enthusiast will be off and running and he or she might talk for ten minutes.

How can you find out these special interests of others? Again a few leading questions usually do the trick.

"When you're not at cocktail parties, what's your favorite form of recreation?"

"If you didn't have to work for a living, what is the one subject in which you would be most interested?"

"If you could do anything you wanted to do, what would it be?"

One of these three questions usually will dig into the other person's favorite special interest. Maybe a truck driver dreams of going to Paris and attending cooking school. Maybe a ballet dancer has always wanted to teach in primary school but never got the college degree. You'll often be amazed and delighted by the special interests that people have, and how eager they are to talk about them.

"Yes, I'm only a secretary now, but I'm trying to turn in my high heels and dresses for fatigues, an M-16 rifle and a pocket full of C-4 plastique. I want to be the first woman soldier for hire mercenary."

By getting the other person to talk about themselves, they will be pleased and happy with you. A good listener is hard to find these days. Everyone loves to talk about themselves and their dreams and exploits. Once you can find this button and push it, you won't have to worry about keeping your conversation going.

Let's say you want to talk about your own special interests to the other person. Maybe he didn't have any, or you couldn't find out what they were and the conversation is dragging. Give it a shot in the arm by presenting one of your own special interests. How?

"Phil, you may not believe this, but I've always wanted to drive a truck, you know one of those sixteen wheelers that runs coast to coast and pulls in at truck stops, and the driver uses a CB radio and tells raunchy jokes with the boys at the diner."

Chances are no matter what your special interest is Phil will have some comment, and now it's your turn to keep the wheels rolling on the conversation by telling him more of your special dreams and employment fantasies.

If you can hit a special interest the same as another person, the sparks will fly the way they did with the movie buffs above. Shared common interests are one of the reasons people becomes friends, date and perhaps even get married.

A good hostess will try to pair up people this way. A hostess might say:

"Gwen, I want you to meet Phil. I know Gwen is into jumping horses, and I understand that Phil has three champion jumpers that go on the circuit every year."

Whammo, we have a match, folks, and the conversation could go on for hours, followed by a tour of the horse barns, and some late night riding and who knows, maybe an early breakfast at some all night eatery near the Interstate.

5. READ THE PAPERS, WATCH TV:

"All I know is what I read in the newspapers," is the way the great American humorist Will Rogers used to put it. Sometimes that's enough.

If you want to be able to keep a conversation going with almost anyone you meet, one of the best ways is to know what's going on in the world, the country, and in your own state and town. The newspapers, news magazines, and TV news and commentaries are some of the best ways.

During some big international incident, it's always good that you can have enough facts about it to carry on a half way intelligent conversation.

"I agree. Eventually the Cuban economy is going to get so bad that the people will rise up and throw out Castro and Communism the way they have all over the world. Cuba and China stand as the last of their breed."

The wider your reading, the wider a circle of friends you'll be able to talk to intelligently. You'll be able to hold your own in the conversation, and encourage the other person to respond with his opinions and views.

One caution. As with most conversations, if you want

them to stay friendly, give a double passing lane's space around politics and religion. These are two topics people don't discuss, they argue and fight about, so stay away from them, and if they come up, quickly steer the conversation back to the weather or the number of marriages that Liz Taylor has had or what the current NBA record is for making consecutive free throw in non playoff games. In short, anything is better to talk about than politics and religion.

Remember that the best way to keep a conversation going is with a combination of each person talking and listening. If it gets too one sided, it's no longer appealing to both parties. Caution yourself if you realize that you're monopolizing the conversation.

One good way to stop doing this is to ask the other person what she thinks about the current topic or about another one. That way you'll stop talking and let the other person carry the load for a while.

As you continue the converstion, you'll find that you're exchanging a lot of information. People who meet for the first time do this almost automatically. You're trading opinions, ideas, facts, where you work, where you live, and as the talk continues, you can start to form opinions about the other person.

There is no more natural way to get to know someone new, and in that way you can determine if you wish to know that person better.

So be aware of how even the information exchange is as you go along. If you feel you're talking too much, ask an open ended question and then encourage a longer response from the other person. Some ways to do this are to ask why the person thinks this way, or how he came to this conclusion, or perhaps where and how he grew up, and how well he likes the new state or area.

Above all, remember that the balanced conversation is one that will keep going and allow both parties to get to know each other better.

6. KNOW HOW TO LAUGH:

Almost all comedians make it a habit to use themselves the butt of their jokes. They laugh at themselves and at their spouses and their families. People enjoy listening to a person who can make them laugh, but if the comic is laughing at himself, somehow it's that much funnier.

The same thing can apply in conversation. Inject humor into this ongoing conversation when it's appropriate. If you can even tell a joke on yourself, it makes it that much better. Too often humor is cruel, and the cruel joke needs a victim. If you tell an ethnic joke, you almost surely will be insulting someone.

The joke on yourself is safe. Nobody can complain about it. Even if you're telling an Irish joke, say, and you're Irish, then the joke is on you, somehow, and not on any other Irishman.

Sexual humor is usually an easy way to get a laugh, but all too often sexual humor is offensive to people. The cheapest type of humor is the dirty-word syndrome humor. It's where many comedians start and where the poor ones finish. So when you try to inject humor into a conversation to lighten it, tell a joke on yourself, or some inoffensive one that will not upset the person you're talking with.

Try this one:

"I was standing in line at the ticket counter in Brussels last week and a truly Ugly American was ahead of me. He brow beat the clerk. He insulted her. He was loud and offensive. He wound up scolding her because she didn't get the window seat he wanted. Then he left in a huff asking to see her supervisor.

"When I came to the window I told the clerk I was an

American, too, and we all weren't like the man just ahead of me. I apologized for his crass, insulting behavior.

"The sweet little clerk smiled and nodded. Then she said. "Mr. Jones is going to Los Angeles, right?" I had overheard that much of the conversation.

"Don't worry about him. I'm sending his luggage to Brazil!"

7. NEVER INTERRUPT:

One conversation problem almost everyone hates is being interrupted. We all do it from time to time, but try as best you can NEVER to interrupt someone else who's talking.

It is basic rudeness. It shows a lack of respect for the rights of the other person. It shows that you are so wrapped up in what you believe, that you aren't even listening to what the other person is saying.

In a conversation with a new acquaintance, you must be on your best speaking behavior. Don't talk too loud, or too long. NEVER interrupt.

One way to do this is to concentrate on exactly what the person is saying. Repeat it silently in your mind as it's being said. Then think through what it means. If it's a contradiction to what you believe, you might want to start working up some opposing statement that won't be jarring or impolite.

Some people hold their breath if they are anxious about interrupting. This works. It's hard to talk when you're concentrating to hold your breath.

In the end, it's just a matter of being courteous and let the other person have his say, then you can have yours. Remember, you've been trying to get this guy or girl to talk for the last ten minutes, and now he or she is off and running. So don't interrupt. You might not be able to get him jump started again.

8. INTERPRETIVE LISTENING:

Another way to keep a conversation going is by interpretive listening. By this I mean you must be able sometimes to read between the lines. People don't always say EXACTLY what they mean. Sometimes you need to be alert and interpret what you think the person means. But don't act on that interpretation. Rather recast the person's statement through your interpretation and restate it to them.

All this means is simply telling the other person what his statement means to you. For example:

"I really don't like this party," Phil said.

"Are you telling me you feel uncomfortable because you don't know enough people here?" Gwen asked.

Phil grinned. "That's exactly what I mean but I wasn't sure why I was so uncomfortable until you translated it for me. Why don't we join forces and see if together we can meet everyone in the room before the party is over."

Here Gwen could have snapped back. "If you don't like it here, why don't you leave." Instead she tried to figure out why he was unhappy, hit it right on the head, expanded her friendship with Phil and together that night they did meet almost everyone at that party.

9. ALWAYS BE ENTHUSIASTIC:

Everytime you're talking with someone, remember to be alert, bright eyed and enthusiastic. If you are, everyone will be glad to talk with you. Your enthusiasm gives them the signal that you are alive, that you're alert and interested in what they're talking about.

This helps to keep a conversation going. You can help show your enthusiasm by nodding when they say something that you agree with, by keeping eye contact and by making appropriate remarks.

When you respond to what they say through your own input into the information pool, that also helps to keep the conversation going.

The longer two people talk, the more they find out about each other, and that can lead to a decision:

"Do I want to stay with this turkey and get more bored and out of circulation, or shall I chuck him/her and go find another person who might be more interesting?"

What we're talking about now, is how can you end a conversation. Just walk off? It might not be that easy. To find some great ideas on this touchy subject, turn to the next page.

4

HOW TO END A CONVERSATION

Time to bug out, *sayonara, hasta la vista*, bye bye baby, so long, see you around, graduation time. This girl you've been talking with looked great, but after five minutes of trying to carry on an intelligent conversation with her, you at last realize that she's not an imitation of a fence post, she is a real live cedar fence post. How do you end the conversation politely, naturally and without upsetting her?

Remember the song, FIFTY WAYS TO LEAVE YOUR LOVER? Well, don't get excited, we don't have quite that many, but there are a number of tried and true methods you can use to get away from a dead-end conversation quickly and with no screaming and no pain.

Even a talk with a bright, witty person is going to come to an end sooner or later. Let's look at some good ways to get moving.

1. EXITING A GOOD CONVERSATION:

Let's talk about that good, positive conversation that you've been having. Interesting person, but you've about run out of things to say and it's time to stop. This is the point to do it before either of you start to struggle trying to keep things going or when you both are looking into your drinks and wishing you were somewhere else.

If you want to see the other person again, this would be the time to set up a date. If it's just a casual talk, you might say:

"George, I understand how you feel about the homeless situation, and I'll certainly try and find that article you mentioned in the Sunday paper. It was good talking with you, I bet that we'll run into each other again."

With that hold out your hand, shake it politely nod and turn away to the rest of the room and you're off on a new hunt for someone to talk to.

In this kind of a good bye, you have repeated the person's name so you'll remember them easier the next time. You've left a good impression with them by remembering it. You've spoken about George's pet project, the homeless, and you've scored some points there by saying you'll learn more about the problem.

2. LEAVING A BAD EXPERIENCE CONVERSATION.

You knew three minutes into the talk with this couple that it was not going to be to your liking. They were experimentalist when it came to law and order, you suspect that they are high on drugs, and sometimes they don't make sense. How to get away from this pair without them causing a scene?

Here you simply have to be honest and businesslike. If the people are talking their heads off, you need to wait until there's the hint of a pause, then you bore in with a couple of ideas of your own. You might want to say, "I really don't agree with you on this point, but this is a democracy."

41

You might look across the room and wave. "Oh, would you mind if I left you for a while? I just saw Madeline over there and I need to talk to her. It's been interesting chatting with you and we'll probably see each other again."

Shake their hands, use their name in your goodbye's and turn and walk away.

If you really don't have someone else to go talk to, slide over to the bar and get another drink, or hit the food table. The couple might think you're getting something for a friend. Chances are as soon as you leave, the couple will be looking for another victim to corner and they won't even watch you.

The quicker you can find someone with an open stance who will make eye contact and smile, the better. Zero in on them and talk, if even for a few minutes, to reinforce the small lie you told to unhitch yourself from the couple's wagon.

3. SIGNALS AND HINTS TO USE TO END IT:

There are a few generally recognized signals you can use when you're getting ready to end a conversation. Most people recognize them and will be prepared.

If you're sitting down, the major sign is for you to stand. This is a universal signal in business and in society that the talk is over, bye bye, we're out of here.

Another highly effective method of indicating you're about to move, is to break eye contact. Say you've been working hard at maintaining eye contact for most of your talk. Now you want to leave, so you break off the eye contact and look off in another direction.

I've seen people start looking at their watch every minute or so. This is a sure sign that time is passing and the person wants to be on the move.

Some smooth talkers will use the summary or recap method to send the signal. They recap the key points the other person has been making, perhaps say again some of their own major thoughts on the subject. Then they might say:

"Well, George, it's been an interesting exchange of viewpoints. We don't always agree. Voltaire had something to say about that. I've enjoyed talking with you, George. Perhaps we can do this again sometime."

Then you nod, smile and walk away.

Usually it's a good idea not to lie to the other person especially if you don't want to see them again, and don't want to meet them for lunch downtown, and don't want to come to their next party. In this case say you enjoyed the talk, shake hands and leave.

4. THE HARD TO HANDLE AND DIFFICULT:

What if a drunk latches onto you? Say a Jennifer grabs your arm and leans against you and starts talking and simply doesn't want to let go. If you let go of her she'll fall down.

How can you deal with this?

The hostess or host should be watching for such people and take care of them for you. If the person is a friend of the hostess, she would be the first to see the problem and help out Jennifer.

If the hostess doesn't arrive, one interesting way to ditch Jennifer is to take her to an empty chair, sit her down and go get a drink for her. Make it Perrier and when you bring it back, hand it to her and then use one of the exit lines.

"Jennifer, I think you'll find it simpler to sit there a few minutes. It's been interesting talking with you, but I do have to go back to the bar and refresh my drink. You be good now and take care." You're off and on your way.

A belligerent or loud person who might also be drunk or on drugs is especially difficult to deal with. If that person has picked you out to be the recipient of his scorn or his loud talk, you have a big problem.

I've seen whole groups of people move away from such an individual. If you are the pin pointed target, do your best to be polite and civil. In this case you always have the option of simply turning your back on the man or woman and walking away and getting others between you.

The belligerent one will forget you as soon as you're out of range of his bleary eyes and he'll find a new victim. Hopefully the host or whoever is running the meeting or program will find the distracter and usher him off the premises.

5. ESCAPING THE SHOULDER CRYER:

You've seen them, the person who simply wants to cry on your shoulder for the rest of the evening. Perhaps they are miserable or had some bad luck or just got fired or lost a big sale or were divorced or suffered some financial setback. Nobody wants to be the one to listen to this continual sad tale of woe.

If you're skilled enough, try to break into the sad story and ask the person some simple closed end questions. With you asking the questions you can control and channel the conversation out of the weeping and moaning, and get it onto something that could be productive.

Often this kind of a person will perk up if you show interest in the answers to the questions he or she gives. It could be just enough to pull the individual out of the depression at least for a while, then you can enjoy a normal conversation.

If nothing works, break eye contact, look around at someone else, and use your get away line.

"Well, Paul, I'm sorry about your troubles, but I've got a few of my own to worry about. You take it easy and I hope things work out for you. I really need to go over that way and see a friend."

Say goodbye and walk.

6. GET AWAY FROM A HIGH PRESSURE TALKER:

We've all been in a conversation we wanted desperately to get out of. Anything would do, just get us away from this individual.

This can happen lots of ways: a fast talking political extremist who corners you at a party, a religious fanatic at your door, a high pressure salesman in a car showroom, a sleek and slick telephone salesman who has a response for your every "no." There are dozens more, but this is the type of talker who we want to escape from with only a few of our clothes in shreds.

Over the years, I've found the one solid almost never fail solution to the persistent salesman.

"You have a good product but I can't afford it right now, not even if you cut the price by fifty percent. I don't have any credit and no cash."

The no money excuse is usually the only one that a salesman has not been trained to counter. He knows all of the other solutions to the "no" reasons, but there just isn't one to the idea that you can't pay. That means the company doesn't get any money which translates into the cold fact that the salesman won't get any commission. Period, end of conversation.

Another way to put off a never-take-no-for-an-answer is the stuck record that keeps saying the same few words over and over. In this case you'll use that idea this way:

"I can't buy your product right now, but thanks for your time." When the sales person shows you some more features of the product, say again: "I can't buy it right now, but thanks for your time." After the third or fourth repetition of the phrase it will sink into the sales person's head and he or she usually will back off and look for a live prospect.

What if you're at a party and the person you're talking to is so wrapped up in the local baseball team that he can talk of nothing else. You have pointed out that you're not a fan, you never played, you don't want to know anything about baseball and the local team is so unimportant in your life-scope that it's comparable to the newspaper that goes on the bottom of the bird cage — or kitty litter.

Still he keeps spouting batting averages, reasons why the team is only 48 and 61 at this point in the season and the failure of the short term relievers in the last three weeks due to the flu, injuries and one ace reliever's father died.

How do you escape?

This turkey won't respond to the usual "getting ready to leave" signals. He won't notice when you break eye contact because his vision is clouded with home runs and kicking dirt on the umpire. He won't even notice that he's doing all of the talking. He's in love with his team and with anyone who talks about it. He may not even notice when you stand up.

If you can get a word in between his balls and strike calls, try to say something like this:

"Well Mr. Ty Cobb, it's certainly been fun listening to you talk about the team. But I'm afraid the manager has just pulled the plug on me and is sending in a long term relief pitcher. Then the umpire took offense at what I said as I walked by him and he thumbed he into the showers, so I have to leave. Keep swinging that old hickory." With that kind of a get-away, you should at least get his attention. His eyeballs might even unglaze a minute, but don't worry, he'll nail another listener within half an inning and be back at it again before he gets the signals from the catcher.

With some of the crude, vulgar or unfriendly types, you don't have to worry about being polite to them. I've heard a batch of "bug-out" lines that can do the job here.

"In your dreams, half brain."

"Not on the coldest night in Alaska."

"Get lost, creep."

"Does your mother know you're out without your diaper on?"

"Kiss off, horse face."

"You've got your language training mixed up with your toilet training."

I'm sure you can create a few hundred more. It's always handy to have one or two pet "bug-out" lines like this memorized for instant use. At almost every gathering you'll find at least one creep who needs to be put down. Sometimes a loud voice and distinct enunciation as you point at the person, works wonders.

7. SORRY, WRONG NUMBER:

Now, what about the person you're talking to who is pleasant, but just not your type, or you are bored to death. You don't want to insult him, but you do want to move on to somebody else.

Here you can use the signals. Break eye contact and look around the room. Begin to reply less and less in your conversation exchange. Even allow a little pause before you come back with your answer to a question.

As a final break-away, stand or take a step back and hold out your hand.

"Guinevere, it's been interesting talking to you here in the castle. Right now I need to get over there and see Arthur or I'm going to be in big trouble. Please excuse me." Shake hands with Guinevere and head for the meeting at the big round table.

8. *SAYONARA* LINES ON THE JOB:

Getting away from somebody in a social situation is easy compared to doing the same thing at your work place. Here you have to work with the same people and maintain good relations with them and with your supervisors and bosses for years. How can you tell a supervisor that he's taking up so much of your time that you can't get your work done?

Usually the supervisor won't realize that he's infringing on your work time. His job is to see that you get your work done. But in doing this he often can put the wrong kind of pressures on you to help him with some of his needs.

Let's say that your immediate superior has been given the job of coming up with a way to cut his department's work force by five percent and at the same time increase efficiency.

You're the first one he comes to for some ideas. You talk for an hour and then realize that you are behind in your own work. You need to get out of the spot somehow. What do you say?

Try to turn your problem with time, into his problem.

"Boss, I've given you about all the ideas I have. Now I have to get my own work done."

"Good, good. But just a half hour more. I want to pursue that idea you had of sharing jobs by part timers."

"Tomorrow, Bill. Remember, this is Friday. The Friday report from me to you is due at noon, and then your Friday report is due to your boss by two P.M. How can you get your weekly report ready, if you don't let me get mine ready for you?"

48

"Uh, oh, yeah. Okay, I'll get to work on my weekly report and you keep thinking about this cut back."

"Sure thing, Bill, Now I've got to get to work or I'm going to get fired!"

They both chuckle but Bill gets out of the office so our long suffering hero can get back to work. They're still friends.

Co workers can be murder in this respect. I used to work in a large audio-visual production house where we had fifty writers. There was lots of office hopping and visiting. Often a writer had just finished a script or an assignment and he came in and dropped into the chair beside my desk.

Production *on my assignment* stopped cold dead. We talked for a while and I kept looking at my watch and pushing back to the typewriter. Bob wouldn't leave. I made all the moves and finally I simply had to say to him this:

"Look, Bob. I like to talk to you, and the story about your family vacation should be made into a movie, but I've got a deadline on this first script and I'm two days behind. I just can't talk right now."

Bob jumped up like a poked rabbit. "Hey, why didn't you say so. I hate it when somebody does that to me."

He shot out of my room. I closed the door, hung out my "Do Not Disturb Unless You're Repaying Me Money," sign and got back to work on the script.

Sometimes in equal on equal, even in the business world, a straight forward plea to get out of the office and let you get back to work can turn the trick.

In almost any situation in the business world, when you're in a long conversation with a co-worker or a boss, you can use the tried and true method of getting away. That's to point out that you have a lot of work to do, and you're running out of time. Remind them that time is money and in this case it's going to be your money if you don't get the work done. Your boss and your co-workers can understand this.

So, now we have seen a few ways to get out of a conversation that we really don't want to be saddled with in the first place.

Let's take a step backward and spend some more time on a point that was brought up briefly in a previous chapter. That's how most people can use a few simple methods to help them remember names.

How to do that? First remember to turn to the next page and then start reading.

5

HOW TO REMEMBER PEOPLE'S NAMES

Most of us can think of times when we haven't been able to remember someone's name. It might be a person we met five minutes ago or a friend we have known for years. There is no mystery to remembering names, it just takes some know how, some practice and the desire to make sure we don't forget names.

This isn't talking about the showman who can stand up forty people in the audience, go down the line and have them tell him their names, then go back to the start of the line and name everyone correctly. That's a special skill, a highly developed talent but that person, too, uses some of the methods that we're going to talk about.

One of the bad examples that comes to mind happened in the days of the big rich movie studios when the stars were all contracted for seven years and were virtual slaves.

One young starlet was introduced to the head of the studio at a dinner and an hour later she called him by the wrong name. That young starlet remained a starlet. She had not remembered the name of the king of the studio and did little work after that.

The poor little starlet simply wasn't *concentrating* on the person's name when she was introduced. There are many reasons why people don't concentrate when they meet

51

someone new.

They might be worried about how they look or what the other person will think of them. They may be thinking of something bright and witty to say and not concentrate on remembering the name. They may be nervous if the individual they are meeting can have a big part in their life with things like promotions, employment, social status.

What we're going to show you here will all come down to one simple rule: Be concentrating when introduced. Don't let yourself be distracted. Your job is to listen, understand, know for absolutely certain what the person's name is the moment that you are introduced.

Make sure that you are not distracted, worried, thinking about something else, excited, anxious, wondering about what the other person will think of you. Above all, don't be trying to think up some witty remark for the occasion.

Repetition is one of the basics of all learning, so we're going to do a little repetition here. To help you remember names of those introduced to, and others you want to remember:

I. CONCENTRATE AT AN INTRODUCTION:

Concentration is your first and most important job. Even if you are ill or sweating or unkempt or about to lose your glasses, CONCENTRATE on the name of the person you are meeting. One great way to do this is to smile and say:

"My what an interesting name, Van Brocklin. Is that a name of Dutch derivation?"

"Yes it is, my great, great grandfather came from Amsterdam."

"Then the name is spelled with a space after the Van and a capital B on Brocklin?"

By taking time to learn how to spell the name, you have

52

accented the name in your own mind. Now, Van Brocklin will be easier for you to remember.

If there's some distraction, such as loud music or someone laughing or coughing and you really didn't hear the name, don't fake it. Simply say:

"I'm sorry the music drowned us out there for a moment and I didn't hear your name. What was it again?" When you do this be sure to put on a great smile and you might still be in the act of shaking hands with the person and have already said your own name.

When the person repeats his or her name, CONCEN-TRATE on it and make sure that you hear it well and understand the name. If you're ever introduced to actress Swoosie Kurtz, be sure to ask her how she got such an interesting name. That's one that you're sure to remember and you won't get her mixed up with three or four other Swoosies you know.

2. REPEAT THE PERSON'S NAME THREE TIMES:

The old series of three really helps here. Always try to repeat the person's name aloud in conversation three times before your talk is over. Do it once when you shake hands.

"Well, Swoosie Kurtz, I've admired you on the stage, now I'm so happy that you're in the TV series "SISTERS"."

Once during your conversation work her name into the dialogue. Then when you are saying goodbye, repeat her name again so it will stick tighter in your memory. This three-play repetition of the newly introduced person is one of the best ways to help you remember Swoozie Kurtz's name. It isn't the only one.

So for openers you're going to CONCENTRATE on the person's name as you're being introduced, and then after that you're going to REPEAT THE NAME at least three

53

times as you are talking in that first two or three minutes.

3: PICTURE ASSOCIATION:

Now here is how the amazing 40-names-in-a-row showmen do their little trick. They use a finely honed PICTURE ASSOCIATION with each name. They concentrate on it just a moment as they hold the hand of the person introduced to them. Then they move on to the next one.

A picture association is a simple hallmark or characteristic or visual tag that helps them remember the name. The most obvious one to remember for Howard Redding would be, "red." That's because Howard just happens to have red hair. You associate Howard Redding with his red hair.

You can do this whenever you're introduced to someone. As you take their hand and repeat their name, dig out a PICTURE ASSOCIATION tag. It might be anything that will help you remember the persons and tie in the tag with his or her name.

Her name is Mary Johnson and she's a cut up with a merry little face and wit. Make this one Merry Mary Johnson and you have her tagged.

Maybe the next guy is tall and slim and his name is Silas White. You remember how tall and thin the silos were at your grandfather's farm. So you come up with the association of Silo Silas White. Tall and thin and you've nailed down another name.

Try to work out a PICTURE ASSOCIATION tag for the people as you meet them. Usually this won't be more than four or five or maybe six or eight names that you really need to remember in one night.

The idea mentioned before about having a small notebook or pad of paper and writing down the name and now the PICTURE ASSOCIATION Tag, will be another way to make a record of the names for future listing.

Remember that these PICTURE ASSOCIATION tags do not have to be complimentary. No one will ever know them besides yourself. If you meet a rather hefty lady named Frances, feel free to tag her as Fat Frances, and you won't forget the name. Maybe you meet someone named Tom Winter. You already know another Tom, so you might make this one Tom-TWO. You met him on a cold day outside so he's Tom-Two-Cold, which comes back as Tom Winter. Corny, sure. You didn't come up with the same clues for tags that I did? Fine. Each person can work up the PICTURE ASSOCIATION tags that *will remind him* of the person he's concerned with.

Let's say you're in a meeting and there are four people there you don't know. They are Bill, Anne, Ned, Evelyn. How can you hope to remember all four? You don't have time to even say hello to them before the meeting starts and then it's all business.

Remember them as a group. Take the first letters from their names and try to make a word out of it. I rigged this one. What word comes to mind easiest? B-A-N-E, bane, right. Say the group had different names not so easy. Maybe Bill, Wanda, Harry and Andy.

What can that make? Play anagrams on your pad. In this meeting you do have a big pad, so write down their names as fast as you hear them. Just first names will do for now if it's an informal meeting.

So you have the last four names. The anagram could be WAB-H. That would be for Wanda, Andy, Bill and H for Harry. The words you make up don't have to make any sense, except to you. The word chain can be fun to work with, especially if you have a little time.

We mentioned a name associated with "FAT" a little ways back in this chapter. Do you remember the name? Fat who? Fat Francies, right. This is what some people call taking a newly met individual and picking out one memorable or outstanding feature of that person and using that as the tag.

We did that when we used Fat Frances, and Red Redding. Carry it a step farther. As soon as you meet someone, grab at an outstanding feature. Say he's got great buns and tight pants and he's a hunk anyway and his name is Harold. You can call him Buns Harold or even Buns Hunk Harold. Nice way to remember the guy, right? You won't forget those buns!

Let's say a woman is on your meet list tonight. She's wearing a slinky black party dress that someone poured her into. It's so tight you can count her ribs and see her nipples. No matter what her name is her tag is Slinky. Her name happens to be Mackintosh, but I'd still call her Slinky Mackintosh because of that dress and her great figure.

Free association is one of the best ways to remember a person's name. Be sure that as you're doing this you follow the other points: Concentrate, repeat the name, then work the picture association.

4: FAMILIAR NAMES:

One more way to help you remember names doesn't apply to all names. Those familiar ones, the more widely used ones, might spark an immediate association with another person.

You meet Paul and he reminds you of your uncle Paul, so right away you have a good tie.

Another person might be large and heavy and not terribly attractive and be the perfect match for your Aunt Matilda.

A new acquaintance might look like your boyfriend in high school, Jerry, and you'll never forget his name. So this is Jerry-high school. Bingo, you've nailed down another one.

5: THE POLAROID SYNDROME:

Some people use a slightly different method of remembering names. They pretend they have their Polaroid camera and take an immediate mental picture of the person. This requires a quick study by you, a careful eye for detail, and a logical memory pattern.

A man walks in and he's a true hunk, with a big smile, a sport shirt bulging with muscles, an attractive face and he's at least six-four and a muscled 190 pounds. What's not to like. So you shoot your mental/Polaroid. Green eyes, tended brows, a fine head full of brownish-red hair a little long and shaggy. No glasses. A strong nose and a chin you could break rocks on. Now you have a fine mental picture of Bryon. Whenever you want to remember B-R-Y-O-N, dig out this picture from your mental hard file of bytes and there he is, Bryon in all of his muscled, Greek God glory.

6: THE MEMORY CRUTCH:

Having a good memory for names and faces isn't as hard as most people believe. That's because most of us don't work at trying to remember. If you follow the ideas in this chapter, your memory of names and faces should improve by 100 percent.

It isn't hard to remember. What is important is that you have to remember to try to remember. Concentrate on introductions when they come. Dig into the five or six methods of memorizing a person's face and their name, and you'll be surprised. Just repeating a person's name three times during an introduction and short talk will do wonders.

The key to a good memory is the effort you put into

it. Some people have fantastic memories, or so it seems. Some can remember bits and pieces of conversation five years later.

A man surprised me one day. I hadn't seen him in eight years and when we met again he remembered my name, my wife's name and asked us how our son was who had cancer surgery. We got to be good friends after that and I asked him how he did it.

He said he used all of the methodology of remembering names, and he worked hard at it. He said probably the thing that helped him the most was that he genuinely was interested in people and he cared for them. That was how he remembered my son's operation. He said he had wondered since, how my son came out of the surgery and what he was doing now.

CARING is the key word here. If you CARE for someone, you'll be able to remember the name. The reverse is also true. If you have no interest in a person and don't care if you ever see or hear from them again, chances are that you'll subconsciously blot out their name as well and move on to more pleasant memories.

7: REMINDERS FOR REMEMBERING NAMES:

• Smile, shake hands and gain eye contact.
• Concentrate on the person's appearance and name.
• Be sure you hear the name, and repeat it at once.
• If you didn't hear the name, ask the person to tell you again and be sure you know it.
• Try to associate this name with someone you know.
• Do a picture association of this person, pegging some outstanding feature with her name to spur your recall.
• Repeat the name out loud at least three times during your talk.

- If you forget the name, don't be afraid to ask the person again. Say you want to be sure to remember the name exactly right.
- Concentrate on the other person you're meeting, not about yourself or what you're wearing or what to say next.
- Care about the person you're meeting. This is another human being with hopes and fears and loves and sadness. Remember the whole person, but tag him or her with one feature.

This should be one of the most thumbed, heavily read sections of the book. Remembering names is vital in our modern society, especially if you're in business. The salesman who remembers your name after a year is going to be much better welcomed than the one who doesn't.

You will be welcomed warmly in both social and business situations when you remember and use a person's name when meeting and greeting and conducting your business.

Now that we've taken care of the remembering part, let's move on into some of the ways that you can utilize these newly found tools of conversation.

Let's say you're having a small party. How can these conversation methods help you be more at ease and have a successful event? How? Turn to the next chapter.

6

PARTY CONVERSATIONS

When many people think of a party, they think of a group of people sitting or standing around talking. The cocktail party is almost purely social, and the biggest event at most of them is the chatter among the guests.

Almost all except the strictly structured parties have a large element of casual conversation. That means it's at parties where you'll be able to perfect your new attitude toward and your new skills in the gentle art of conversation.

TALKING AT YOUR OWN PARTY:

Giving your own party is something some people shy away from. They say they don't know how, they are uncomfortable, and they wouldn't know how to talk to people.

With what you've just learned about the art of conversation, giving your own party should be a breeze. Let's take a look at some practical applications of the conversational methods and techniques that you've just learned to see how they work in your own party situation.

First, *don't overplan and don't worry*. Lots of people get up tight and nervous about giving a party, worrying that each individual aspect must be honed to perfection from the lighting right down to the type of forks used and the snacks that are set out for the guests.

If you don't plan too much, there will be less for you to worry about. The purpose of your party, let's say, is to introduce some of your new friends to some of your older friends. A simple little affair with maybe twenty people in your home.

Remember, part of your purpose in this party is a practical one — so your new friends can get to know more people in your circle and that will help them and your other friends both socially, on a personal basis and perhaps even professionally as well.

Generally think that your job as host or hostess is to make everyone feel comfortable and at ease. Make them pleased that they came and show them that you are happy they could be there. This is a lot easier to do that at first it might seem. It starts with your guest list.

What you're trying to do is invite people who know most of the others and who are good talkers, so there won't be a single moment of total silence. Some people are better at conversation than others, so pick and choose.

A rocket scientist might be brilliant, but you won't invite him because if he did come, he'd probably spend the whole evening sitting in the corner glaring at the other guests, wishing he was home working on his next theory about warp drive so he can get his rockets all the way to the stars within his own lifetime.

Be sure everyone meets everyone else. One of your major jobs at your own party is to make sure that everyone there has met everyone else. It's frowned on by the social set, but the use of name tags isn't at all out of place. If half of the people know each other, that still leaves a huge name gap.

Pre-printed stick on name tags can be a boon to any host or hostess.

When the first of your newcomers arrive at your party, be sure that you are at the door to welcome them. If the weather permits it's a great idea to leave the front door open. Then welcome each guest and make sure the new people are introduced by you to each of the other people who have arrived.

Later on this may be more difficult, but whenever you have the chance, lead your newer couples around and let them meet as many of the people as possible.

Any time you can give a little background on the people it is a large help.

"Mrs. Jenkins, this is Dr. and Mrs. Harlowe. Dr. Harlowe is new in town and joining the Scripps Research Center in their new brain wave research project."

Then follow as soon as you can and give some detail about Mrs. Jenkins.

"Dr. Harlowe, I'm not sure if you know it or not but Jane Jenkins is one of the leading defense lawyers in town. She handles a lot of the important cases here."

Introductions with some facts about the parties make it much easier for the people to move on into a conversation that lets the people become more familiar with each other at a more rapid pace than if they must start out with the closed end questions and forge ahead.

That's part of the way you can make your own party a success by encouraging this kind of conversation that gets people to know each other.

From time to time, take a good look around and make a small tour. Spot anyone who is standing alone, or sitting alone, and take someone over and introduce them. Try to keep everyone involved and talking. That's part of your job as the hostess.

Check your seating arrangements: If you have a sit down dinner, make sure that you think carefully before assigning the seats. Don't put a young bachelor between two older well-married women. They probably will be delighted to talk with him, but he's going to be much happier at least with one dinner partner who is attractive and available.

Your seating chart should be the biggest impetus to conversation that you have. Our rocket scientist won't be there, but another lawyer might be interested in sitting next to the defense council mentioned before. The architect might have something in common with the builder, and the ballet dancer will be more pleased to talk with a musician than with a man who makes surfboards for a living.

Try to think about conversations between these people as you work out your seating arrangements.

If you find a few people at your party with "closed stance" and a small frown, make it a special point to talk to them and get them into a conversation with someone else. Many people don't realize that they are standing that way and scaring people off. As hostess it's your job to be on the watch for any one who seems to be uncomfortable and get them involved.

Maybe there is a reason for their stance, and you might be able to help with that as well.

When you give a "conversation" party, remember all of the good methods for getting people talking and try to encourage as much friendly chatter as you can.

WHEN YOU'RE A PARTY GUEST:

Let's say you're going to an important party. This is an industry affair where your boss and several management people from your firm will be there, but also there will be dozens of big shots from the same types of business there.

How do you act? Who do you talk to? Should you let your boss see you talking with a rival executive? Will he think you're looking for a new job?

The best thing to do at this kind of an affair is "just don't worry." It's a social situation, not a business forum. No one is hauling out a resume or employment application. If you find you're talking with the president of the biggest firm in town, make the best of it. Shake hands, trade names and make him think you're interested in whatever he says.

If the chance comes up, and you have something important to say about the way the industry is going, or the type of restraints the government is putting on, let it come out. You have a right to your opinion.

Whatever you do, don't tie up and go blank. This is a party, so move around and see how many of the top people you can meet.

Keep all of those basics: have an open posture with no folded arms or hand over your mouth. Smile and make eye contact and be open and friendly. Always, remember the names of those new people you meet. Write them down if you can. Never hurts.

Even if you're available and you meet this gorgeous hunk or this fantastic lady, be sure that you don't spend the whole party talking with that one person.

You might make a date to have lunch in a few days, but it's still part of your job to circulate and keep the party moving. Nothing says that you can't drift back for a second round of talks later on. If you do keep circulating, your host will appreciate it, and who knows, there might be a better prospect in that next group of people around the punch bowl.

At any party, there will be people you know and those you don't. Make it a point not to spend all of your time talking with old friends or fellow workers. Again, circulate and get to know the new folks on the block.

Here you'll go back to the basics and watch for the open stance, the smile and the eye contact. Use the same signals yourself and meet those new people.

Recently I was at a small party held after the opening night of a play. The play was an old standard and delightfully done in an Equity-Waiver theatre in Los Angeles. We met the star of the show and then talked to a few more people. We had a long drive and left after a half hour or so.

On the way home one of the people in the car said: "Did you see Lee Merriweather standing over by the door?"

I hadn't. Then I remembered that Lee Merriweather's husband was one of the actors in the eight person play.

"Why didn't you tell me she was there?" I yelped. "It would have been interesting to meet her."

Our haste in leaving, and not communicating with the others in our own group, meant I didn't get to meet a fine actress and the former Miss America of 1955.

Circulate, try to meet everyone at the party. That's why most people go, to see who's there and to be seen. That's not only true in Hollywood.

SURE, YOU'LL GET STUCK WITH A TURKEY NOW AND THEN:

No matter how lucky you are at parties, sooner or later you're going to get stuck with an absolute loser, a turkey that can't even make it in the Thanksgiving rush.

Many of these people are not mean or cruel or obnoxious. I remember one lady I talked to at a party. She was so withdrawn it was actually painful for her to talk with people she didn't know. But she had to come to the party. It was a gala following a ballet performance.

I tried half a dozen different subjects. On the closed end questions I would get the yes or no answers. The trouble was when I asked her a what or why question, she just smiled and looked at me and then looked away.

Truth was I was getting desperate. The director of the

ballet company had asked me to talk to Maria and be especially nice to her. She was a lady in her forties, slim and trim and so shy it was starting to be painful to me.

Then I asked her if she thought the ballerina in our small company had done justice to the leading role in GISELLE. To my surprise she nodded and began to talk.

Ballet was her life. She had been a ballerina herself in New York until an accident forced her into retirement. Now she went from company to company acting as a special teacher, giving master classes and helping on a production here and there.

She knew ballet, she knew the one the company had performed that night. We talked for half an hour and then I introduced her to some other balletomanes and she continued to talk about the ballet and what the company had done well and what they could do to improve.

At last I slipped away, but I had learned that no matter how shy a person might be, almost all of them will open up if you can find the right topic that's close to their hearts.

Even if a person you're talking to seems to have nothing in common with you, it's your place to make a try at finding something to talk about for five minutes. By asking the why questions you sometimes can dig out a topic that both of you can discuss.

You might even fall back on talking about the hostess or the party itself, or the decorations. It's surprising what might trigger off a response from a person you had been struggling with to get on the conversation track.

WHAT ABOUT THE RUDE, INTERRUPTING AND COLD SHOULDER?

When you meet a rude person at a party, what can you do? It certainly isn't someone with whom you want to carry on a meaningful conversation.

"This is absolutely the worst party I've ever been to," Willy might say. You've been talking to him for five minutes and you seemed to have some things in common but then he blurts this out.

Does he mean he doesn't enjoy talking with you? Is it the food or the drinks? Does he think everyone there are klutzmanics and far below him?

It takes a lot of old fashioned guts to look Willy right in the eye and say: "If you don't like it, why don't you leave?" Challenge him that way. Usually I can't do it and I'd like to. If you can, quite often the person will back down with some kind of a lame excuse:

"I didn't actually mean that, and I don't want you to think I haven't enjoyed talking with you, but I was supposed to meet somebody here and she hasn't come."

So, his real reason came out in the open.

Often when someone is unhappy like Willy was above, many of us will close out the conversation quickly and retreat to a safe harbor of someone we know and can talk with. The challenge is fine if you can handle it.

If you're in a group of three or four talking and you have the floor setting forth your position on something, what can you do when someone breaks in interrupting you?

Again, if you can do it, the best way to handle a rude person such as this is to look them in the eye. "Pardon me, I'm talking here. It's my turn. When I'm through then you can argue all you want to, but give me the courtesy I gave you and let me finish my statement."

This almost always works. It's a not so gentle put down that the person deserves.

I was talking before a group of writers and editors one night and someone asked me about what they could expect to be paid for writing a first novel. I told them that it could be anywhere from five hundred dollars to ten or fifteen thousand.

The questioner was satisfied but the man sitting beside him stood up with his own question. "You write all these books, so how much money do you make a year?"

I paused a moment and stared at him and shook my head. "That's something that I don't talk about. I don't think it's any of your business. So how much money do you make a year?"

The last line brought laughter and a round of applause from the audience who figured it wasn't any of his business how much I made.

Sometimes a person that you're talking to is simply too rude to endure. In those cases, I look him or her in the eye, say without meaning, "Thanks for the talk," and turn and walk away without shaking the person's hand. It's the kind of put down that some people will understand, but some rude people won't even have a hint of why you left so abruptly.

Have you ever been at a party where there's a definite chill in the room? Almost everyone there knows almost everyone else, and they cluster around the room in small groups that don't break up.

You've done your best to "crash" these cliques. You've wandered into the circle, listened, tried to make a comment, but get the cold shoulder and maybe even were cut off in mid sentence by someone else.

The only thing you can do here is try another of the groups. If they all turn out to be the same, maybe your hostess made a mistake and invited you to the wrong group of her friends. The best thing you can do in this case is to find your hostess, tell her you just don't fit in with the people this time, thank her for her kindness and get out of there. There might be a good movie on late night TV or on one of the pay channels, so all is not lost.

THE PARTY'S OVER:

When you leave a party is mostly up to you. If you're having a good time, meeting interesting people, making a few contacts in your networking, and enjoying the food and chatter, stay on.

If you're getting the idea that it's about time to go, the best way is to leave when someone else is going. That way the hostess will be at the door and you won't have to hunt her up to say your good bye.

It's rude and counter productive to leave any party without saying good bye to your host and hostess. Use your best conversation techniques. Smile and make eye contact, and convince your hostess that this was the best party you've ever been to. Thank her for introducing you to her friends, and then shake hands or give her a hug and you're out the door.

Try never to overstay your welcome. If you suddenly realize that it's late and there are only two or three people left at the party, make your exit quickly. Your hostess is probably about ready to drop over from exhaustion.

Always thank your hostess for inviting you and make a note to be sure to invite her to your next small gathering.

Parties, what a great way to spend an evening. Also one of the best times to test out all of your great conversation techniques that will help you meet people and make friends.

Now, let's say that you've been practicing. You have the open stance down, you don't cover your mouth with your hand, and you are great at eye contact over your good smile.

But somehow you seem to run out of things to say after your conversation gets in gear. Are there some other ways, sort of the advanced course, in how to keep a conversation going? Glad you asked. There are and I'm about to tell you about them. First though, turn to the next chapter.

7

ADVANCED COURSE: KEEP THE CONVERSATION GOING

There are a lot of ways to keep a conversation moving after it seems to have stalled. Here are a few that might come in handy on your next dead-engine try to get the talk to continue.

MISINTERPRETED SIGNALS:

Sometimes in a one-on-one conversation a person will misread what the other person says, or misunderstand something and the conversation skids to an abrupt halt and the person who thinks they have been injured turns and walks. The best way to avoid this is not to launch any statements or suggestions that can be misinterpreted. Remember that some people are excessively sensitive about their weight or their height or even a large nose. Be thoughtful and never tease anyone about any physical attribute.

Some people hate their freckles, and women especially may be so concerned about trying to cover up freckles that it becomes an obsession with them.

If you call one a beautiful freckled redhead, she might throw her plate at you and stomp away.

Another way to get into trouble is giving veiled suggestions and hints. It's impossible for most of us to read another person's mind. We don't know what they mean unless they come right out and say it.

The half-way invitation to have lunch or coffee in a day or two is a good example. You might make such a suggestion, and the other person is not sure if it's an invitation or just a toe in the water to test the coldness.

"It might be nice if we could have lunch together sometime," is one of the best ways not to say it. Rather. "I enjoy talking with you. How about our having lunch tomorrow at that little deli near your office on Fourth. We can meet there about twelve-fifteen."

Now the other person has a definite invitation to respond to and doesn't have to wind up making the request.

Remember, if you're making an invitation, be sure it's specific and plain, and never tease someone concerning a subject that they might be self conscious about or get them angry.

THERE'S A TEASE IN EVERY CROWD:

Teasing can have its place. Sub-teenagers use teasing as the first way a boy might ever talk to a girl. Teasing is a way he can approach her and talk without embarrassing himself if she doesn't answer. Kids of all ages use teasing as a safe way to talk with someone else without risk. It's a teen-age trait and serves a good purpose.

In older people, teasing is often used by men who are still a little shy. It's a simple and easy way to start talking to someone and to get their attention.

If teasing is done with a light touch, in good humor and not about some physical characteristic, it usually is one of the slower courting dances of the homo sapiens.

I have a friend who loves to tease. He doesn't go too

far, and the teasing always has a lot of humor and fun in it. He always makes it a positive and caps it off by saying that he only teases people he likes.

Teasing done the right way can help a party along by adding a sense of humor. A good laugh helps things along with most conversations. Remember the comedians who make themselves the butt of their own jokes.

Letting other people tease you and even laughing at, yourself can go a long way to livening up a party and the conversation that you're having. When you're the object of a teaser, take it in good humor and everyone will brighten and the conversations will roll.

SILENCE CAN BE A POTENT WEAPON:

Most good salesmen use silence as a high tech weapon. Say you're talking with a salesman about a new car. He can tell that you want the particular model that he's demonstrating. You ask him about the bottom line price and he makes you a quote.

Then he sits there and waits. He doesn't start caving in and making a better offer. You sit there squirming and remembering the car. You want it. You just thought you could get a better deal.

You start to say something, then stop. You raise your offer on the car by five hundred dollars. All the salesman does it sit there and watch you.

He knows you want the car. He knows that he's given you the best deal he can and still get it approved by the sales manager. After another long dead air time you either give in to his price or stand up and walk out. Usually the salesman wins. He has all the cards.

The same thing works in negotiating with your boss. Make him an offer to do something or ask for a raise and then just sit there and watch him. Silence can be a powerful weapon.

In conversations, it also has its place. A good listener can use silence to his advantage. It's easy to talk, but it's tougher to be a friendly listener. Here silence is great. You can sit there, sip your drink and nod once in a while. Give an "uh huh," now and then and fill in a blank when needed.

Chances are the one who is talking to you will come away from the party and say what a great person you are to talk to, when in reality, he was the one doing most of the talking.

When you're not talking, it also gives you a chance to marshall your thoughts and figure out some new angle on the subject at hand.

Silence can also be used when you don't agree with someone, or when you're trying to get free of a long talker. Try simply not responding, and it's a powerful signal that you want out of the conversation. After a try or two to get you talking or responding some way, the other person will catch on that you simply don't want to talk, and the other person will usually cut and run.

HANDLING CRITICISM:

From time to time we all get criticized in public, in a group and face to face. This is a prime test of your character. How do you respond to criticism where you're trying to keep a conversation going?

You can flare up, challenge the lout to a duel, or if a woman, rush forward and scratch the bitch's eyes out. Neither one a good option. The best way to handle criticism is to leave your defenses down and bring up your sense of humor.

If you can, always try to turn criticism into humor. That takes the importance away from it and helps reduce the sting.

"Charlie, I heard your summation to the jury on that Ascot murder case. That was the worst summation I've ever heard. How in the world did you win that case?" Possible humor take downs on the criticism.

"I tried your tactics, Mort, I bribed a juror." (laughter)

"I knew you were in the courtroom so I had to make my argument simple enough for even you to understand." (laughter)

"I did it just the way you taught me, Mort." (laughter)

Try not to get too cruel when you swipe back at a criticism, but an acid remark like the put downs made above, opens the way for another sharp remark. If you can draw a laugh from the group, it helps take any bitterness out of it and hopefully you'll all still be friends.

Sometimes people will do a gentle put down on you at a party to see how you react. They might not have any malice in mind. In fact, they might be considering you for a job with them, or a new position in your own firm. The better you can handle criticism with good humor, the more you show the detractor that you are sure of yourself, that you are self confident and that you don't consider his criticism as being important.

Sometimes by talking about a bad situation you can defuse it. Say one of your co-workers has ragged you about getting the job to lay out the plans for the new computer network for your company.

You've known the other man for a couple of years and never had any trouble with him. Try and talk it out. Maybe a question will help bring out what's really bugging the person. Try talking to him this way:

"Lew, I don't understand. I put in a bid for the job of making that network just like some others. Did you apply for it, too?"

You find out that Lew did put in his plans. Then the

real gripe comes out.

"You've picked off three assignments that I wanted in the last six months."

Now it's in the open and you can talk about it. Tell Lew maybe he needs to work more on his presentations. Offer to help him with his next one and maybe together they can brighten it up a little bit.

Talking things out usually will smooth the waters and get the animosity out of the situation before it can turn nasty.

NO ROOM FOR ARGUMENTS:

A conversation is no place for arguments. Some people think that they have to be right all the time. No matter what the subject, no matter how much or how little they know about it, they simply insist that they are right about the case.

For this kind of person, a conversation is a challenge, a duel, a contest that he can't stand to lose. He makes every casual talk into a desperation ploy of Intergalactic War III.

The problem here is that this type of person is often insecure and takes the aggressive manner of talking to help him lift his own ego. He in effect says: "If you don't believe what I'm saying, you're stupid."

He might say out loud that your argument is the most stupid thing he's ever heard of.

His conversation is soon going to be one sided, since most of us don't enjoy presenting our thought or opinion, only to have someone tell us that we're stupid for thinking that way. This arguementive-prone person is going to stop most conversations dead in the water between two people and will cast a deadly shadow of silence over a group of five or six.

Taking the reverse attitude is the best way to keep your own conversations going. Have an open mind. Listen for valid arguments and logical deductions. Don't maintain that every opinion you have is absolutely true. A lot of them won't be.

If you believe in something strongly, you have every right to present that opinion. But it never hurts to throw in the phrase: "Of course, that's just my opinion."

This leaves others the right to express their opinion whether it agrees or is at odds with yours, and the conversation rolls along. This way nobody gets upset with anyone else.

If someone else gives their views on the subject and they are about 189 degrees off course from yours, how can you have your say and still keep the conversation going?

One good way is to preface your talk with a softening phrase. These include: "It's been my impression...." or "This is what I believe on that subject..." or "This is the way I see that...." or "It's been my experience in this field..." or simply, "I think...."

This is a soft way to differ with someone, but at the same time you aren't labeling them as stupid lame brains who just got off the turnip truck from the backwoods.

THE WET NOODLE SYNDROME:

Now and then you'll find a complete door mat in a group or at a party. This person seems to take the attitude that he or she can't get in trouble if she never states an opinion and never stands up for some cause.

They think they are safe by just drifting along, becoming a yes-man, not taking any chances, looking a lot like a wet noodle on a hot afternoon in the desert.

Some of these people will deliberately put everyone else's needs ahead of their own. This is one way they can find approval and, they hope, friends.

Usually it doesn't work that way. Friendships are formed

for a lot of reasons but one of them is having mutual respect. How can you respect someone who is a door mat, who cow-tows to every whim of another person and in effect has no thoughts, no principles, no life of his own? Most people can't.

If you even come close to fitting into this category, take a careful look at yourself and at the next opportunity, try to be a little more assertive, stand up for your beliefs, take yourself more seriously. This is the time to have more confidence in yourself. Try it, you'll enjoy it, and the people around you will enjoy being with and talking to you.

Before, I said something about being open minded and ready at least to check out what other people think about a subject. This can be called flexible, but it is not wishy washy. Some politicians are accused of "flip-flops" on issues, usually done when it can bring in a large block of voters. That's not what this is about. Being flexible means that you can change your mind if the evidence dictates it. Being flexible is another way to help you get into and carry on a good conversation.

If you really want to make friends, you need to stand up for what you believe, state your opinion and let others know where you stand, and if there is some decision making to do, promote your cause, take the vote, and then abide by the majority rule. That's what we call democracy. Without standing up for your rights and your opinion, you can't take part in the democratic process.

DON'T BE AFRAID TO ASK:

We all have seen people at parties who declare to the world that they know everything in the human experience. Usually these people are boring. On the other hand there are people who say they know nothing and they are just as bad.

Most of us have opinions about a variety of subjects, and even some special talents and skills. Still there comes a time when we are stumped. If your one-on-one talker of the moment is going deep into some subject that you know nothing about, just push up a red flag and say wait a minute.

"I really don't understand what you're talking about. Could you give me some of the basics about intermolecular space travel and the theory that our whole universe may be a tiny speck in time clinging to the wall of a gigantic black hole that is only a minute part of another cosmos somewhere."

The point is, don't be afraid to ask a question. Don't be afraid to say you don't know what he or she is talking about. I've been a reporter, and talked with people who were so deep into their own subject that they hardly ever used a word that I understood.

It was my job to make the man on the street understand what this guy or woman was saying. Hundreds of times, I've said:

"Now just a minute, you lost me. What does this mean to the average man on the street? Can you explain this so he and I will understand what your field is and what your bright new development in that field is and what it means to us?"

I always got immediate and favorable response. Most experts love to talk about their specialty, about their field. It's their 15 minutes of being famous even if it is for the Weekly Newscope.

Don't be afraid to ask questions. When you question someone about his or her field, it's a compliment. You're saying: "Hey, you're the expert here, tell us common folks what this means."

CHECK YOUR CO-TALKER'S FEELINGS:

As you talk with someone in a one on one or in a group, keep a wary eye out to check to see if the person you're talking to is upset or sensitive about any of the topics that you're discussing. Most people will frown slightly, or even pull back in a chair they are sitting on. Sometimes they revert to the crossed arm syndrome and try to close themselves off from you, even as you're talking.

When you see these tell tale signs, or the indication by their responses that they are uncomfortable discussing birth control or the AIDS epidemic or the distribution of condoms in high school on demand, quickly move to some safer subject.

I remember one woman I was talking to and the subject of adoption came up. One of my friends had just adopted a baby and she was ecstatic. A few moments after I told her about this great adoption, the woman I was talking to excused herself and hurried out of the room.

The hostess came in a few minutes later and hurried over to me.

"What did you say to Beth? She's in the far bedroom crying her eyes out."

It turned out that Beth had just lost a baby two weeks before and the doctor told her that she shouldn't try to have another one. The recall and the reliving of the miscarriage had been too much for Beth.

Watch out for any signs of distress by anyone else in the group as you talk. Usually there is no need to be restrictive in the scope of your conversations. However, once in a while, you'll run into a special case where it's best to change the subject quickly if you have the chance.

Okay, we've had another shot at how to keep that conversation going, even with a difficult or unusual person.

Now let's say you've found a live one, a man or a woman whom you really would like to see again and get to know better. You're available, you know the other person is as well. So how in the world do you tell this person you'd like to see them again?

Most of us do it by issuing an invitation....for coffee, for a drink later somewhere else, for a lunch or a dinner a few days later. You're not good at that sort of invitation giving? That means you need to rush right along, flip over the page and get going on the next chapter.

MAKING AND ACCEPTING INVITATIONS

One vital aspect of good conversation is what happens at the end of it. Does it lead anywhere? Was it a pleasant interlude and nothing more? Or was it the start of what could turn into a friendship, or something even more involved?

The best way to get something like a friendship started is to meet the other person later, next week, Thursday for lunch. We mortals seem to be lacking the skills of mind reading. All we can go by are a few body language signs and the spoken word.

So, let's look at the art of making and accepting invitations. This might be for anything from an appointment for a business get together, to a meet Wednesday for lunch, or a date for the movies, or an opera or a ball game.

GETTING IT ALL STARTED:

Let's say that your conversation is going fine. There are four of you talking, you and your wife and a new friend and his wife. You're about the same age and seem to have some of the same interests.

You have decided this couple would be interesting to invite over for Saturday night.

STOP: Right here is where most people make the first mistake. They pick out something that THEY want to do, rather than try to find out what the other person would like to do. If you're a wild and crazy golfer and you invite the other couple to hit the tee with you at 5:30 A.M. on Saturday, the chances are that you'll get turned down.

Most people don't golf. Most people who do know a little about golf don't want to get up at four A.M. to get to a tee off time of 5:30 A.M.

Take it from the other point of view. What would these new acquaintances of yours like to do. You heard the woman talk about her bridge club. The man said he'd been a car racing enthusiast for years, they both enjoy board games.

Board games. You and your wife love to play Trivial Pursuit, you have three different levels of it.

You now have an activity that all four of you would enjoy.

"Say Carl. How would you and Irene like to come over to our place Saturday night for a game of Trivial Pursuit?"

Now the odds of your getting an acceptance are a thousand times better than if you asked them to play bridge, which Carl hates, or go to the car races, which Irene hates.

The secret for that first contact is to find some social event or activity that you both enjoy.

The same holds true for singles. You've met this hunk who reminds you of a movie star with muscles. In your conversation you've found out that he is single and not involved and that he loves to go to art films.

A new art film from France is opening the next night. Why not make the plunge? What's to lose? You try it:

"Larry did you know there's a new French film opening tomorrow night at the Ken Theatre? I never miss a new one there. Would you like to come with me? My treat."

So, nothing ventured...you know.

TAKE IT NICE AND EASY:

As the old song goes, take it nice and easy. Many times when singles meet and there's the hint of a spark and they decide to see each other again, it should start out slow.

One good way is to meet for lunch somewhere. Not a fancy lunch, maybe a sandwich and a cup of coffee, or even a quick snack at McDonalds where you always go anyway because it's fast and filling.

Just like buying something, it's easier to spend two dollars than it is fifty. The same way with a new acquaintance. You're more ready to gamble a lunch with some pretty lady to get to know more about her, than you are to pop for dinner and a movie and a snack afterwards and a cab ride home. Keep it simple at first.

After the lunch that's in a public place where both of you can feel safe, you might decide that this fine appearing swan you saw at the party has turned into an ugly duckling, and you don't want to waste any more of your best years on her. It's a quick way to find out and cut and run.

On the other hand, if the lunch is the best thing that happened to you all week, and you like the cute little way she grins, and the way she laughs, and you don't mind at all that she has the best figure you've seen since Mindy quit the secretarial pool, you might be ready to take another step along the friendship trail. Maybe a dinner that won't break the bank and then a movie.

One thing about that first date: Be specific. Ask about a specific event (lunch) at a definite time (12:15), and at a specific place (Charlie's Grill on 46th St.) When you ask this way the other person has three definite facts to work with. Maybe her lunch hour is from one to two. So you can adjust the time and you'll take a later lunch.

Maybe she never eats lunch, instead she takes a mile

walk up Broadway and back. It takes her 40 minutes. Hey, who needs lunch anyway, you agree to come along on the walk. (Again a public place where nobody can get in trouble.)

It might be that she used to work at Charlie's Grill and hates the place, so you go to the 46th Street deli instead.

Here's a don't: Don't start out a relationship by asking this way: "Are you doing anything Friday Night?"

Hey, are you trying to embarrass me and making me admit that I'm a stick in the mud and DON'T HAVE A DATE FOR FRIDAY YET? Never start out an invitation in this terrible way. It puts both of you at a disadvantage.

Don't use the world's worst salesman famous line, either: "You don't want to go out with me Friday night, do you?"

The most likely response is to agree. "Of course I don't want to go out with you."

Keep it positive, keep it simple, make it definite in time, place, activity.

GET WITH A GROUP:

Another small and soft way to invite someone out is to use the group technique.

"Bill, a few of us are getting together to have a super bowl party Sunday afternoon. We'd like you to join us at my place."

You remember this woman from a party you were at last week. She's with your firm and works a few floors below you. You didn't think she noticed you and you weren't tremendously attracted to her, but she invited you and it would be a group and you didn't want to watch the super bowl alone, so you say why not and assure her that you'll be there. It's a soft and safe and gentle way to start out with someone and see if you want to get to the "lunch" stage.

HOW TO WORD THAT SPOKEN INVITATION:

There is no one way to word the perfect invitation. It depends on the person and the circumstances. Say you are at a party where there's lots of talk, a little dancing on the patio, good food, some truly funny skits put on by the host and a friend, and then there is this soft spoken, medium sized guy with a lock of wavy hair that keeps falling over his deep brown eyes, and you want to reach over and brush it back so you can see his attractive face better.

He's danced with you twice, and you talked for half an hour at the punch bowl, and now he's sitting beside you and talking about how he's going to write a novel, just as soon as he moves up one more rung on the ladder at the magazine where he's an assistant editor.

You want to see him again, but he hasn't even hinted at it. Why not give it a try? But what to say? What to invite him for? He works just two buildings down from yours. How about lunch? Everyone eats lunch. Well almost. Yes, lunch.

You look over at him and he grins and you almost melt down into a small puddle. Almost, but not quite. You hold your breath, then look him in the eye and smile your best and make the plunge.

"Warren, I've enjoyed talking with you tonight. I have an idea for an article for your magazine. Do you think we could talk about it over lunch tomorrow?"

There, you said it! Not bad, but you'll have to scratch for an idea that would fit into THE FARMER'S HOME LIFE MAGAZINE.

Warren grins and nods. "Mindy, I'd like that. Where shall we meet?"

So you arrange a definite time and place and it's a done deal. You're going to "do lunch!"

WHAT IF YOU GET TURNED DOWN?:

"No."

"Not a chance, Buster."

"In your dreams."

You won't hear many turn downs like these. Usually the person you're talking with has some sensitivity and if they can't go somewhere will at least tell you why.

"Oh, I'm sorry I can't go to lunch with you Tuesday, I'm taking off that day to get some family matters taken care of at home."

Almost always a turn down will be accompanied with a reason why they can't go with you. Most of the time these are true. Some people have prepared turn-down statements all memorized to fit most occasions and reasons that just can't be changed. You won't find many of these, and probably won't recognize them when they are used. Don't worry. Charge on. There are a lot of koi in the pond of life.

From here on, you're on your own. You can try to figure out if the turn down reason is real, and if it sounds like it and the other person is friendly, you might try some other day or some other activity.

"Well then what about Thursday? I want to find out more about you and how you write all of those fantastic articles."

Nice try. If he really was tied up on Tuesday, and wants to have lunch with you, he'll go for Wednesday or figure out a better day.

Changing the kind of a activity you suggest for a date often works wonders.

"Sorry Wilbur, but I just don't like to go bowling. I always throw gutter balls and make a fool of myself."

"Then how about miniature golf. You said you used to be a good golfer. I'd like to try that."

Here you have come back with an activity that the other person has already indicted some interest in, and your chances of getting an acceptance have just zoomed.

THE BIG FREEZE:

If you get a no, without any explanation, it's usually best not to press the matter. More women do this than men. After a no they tend to go into a deep freeze, or ask to be excused, or simply stand and walk away.

Women I've talked to say it's a basic female defense mechanism. Here is someone coming on too strong or too fast, they feel threatened and they jump and run, rather than stay and fight off another invitation.

Men have the same option. When you get a quick no with no reason, the best move on your part is to thank the lady for talking with you, stand and nod and walk away to a better conversationalist. The punch bowl or food table is always a good last resort in this case. You'll probably find other rejectees there as well.

On the other hand, some people are persistent. You've heard of the young man who asked a young lady out and she turned him down. He called her every day and asked her out to all sorts of activities from a cup of coffee to a lunch to dinner to a fantastic concert.

After more than 30 calls the young lady at last said yes to a quick lunch on their noon hour. She was surprised and totally captivated by the young man who had been so persistent. They went out again that weekend and then twice a week and then three times a week and a month later they were engaged.

Sometimes persistence can pay off.

Ask any top salesman. This is in effect what you're doing, trying to make a sale of yourself to get that first date. A salesman might call on a new account for six or eight months before the business man will decide that he's been there so often he should give the poor salesman a token order.

A salesman that persistent is usually a good one and will realize the chance he has. Here is a toe in the door. He'll be sure to give excellent service, perhaps suggest some products new to that field, and generally serve the customer so well that the one time buy, might soon result in getting the whole account.

It's up to the one asking for that first date or first "outside" meeting, whether male or female, to do the same thing. If you find the light of your life who won't even say hello, you have your work cut out, but it's not an impossible task.

All of this started with that first, open stance, that smile, and a friendly hello after eye contact with this sexy black-haired hunk at the office party. He didn't remember your name, passed you twice without a hello, and still you know that he's the man for you. So don't just stand there. Come up with some great ideas to use to get him interested. Maybe he will. Keep hoping, Alice. This sure isn't Kansas, you know.

Next on the agenda: How can we turn all of these fine meeting and greeting and smiling and talking and invitations and all of that sort of thing into making a friend? How? You guessed it by now, turn to the next chapter.

88

9

MAKING FRIENDS

Almost everything that we've talked about up to this point has been basic training for making friends. To make a new friend, you have to meet someone new. The best way to do that is to follow the steps in the chapters previous: You have an open stance, hands away from your mouth, you smile, you make eye to eye contact and you should often be the first one to say hello.

Then you move into starting a conversation techniques and learn how to keep it going and how to handle small problems and then how to ask if you can see someone again.

Basic training. This is how a new friendship starts. Most people don't have enough friends. A lot of people have almost no good friends — ones they can tell their secrets to, their ambitions, their fears. We all need good friends we can confide in.

The one great thing about friendship is that it can start and flourish at any time in life. There is no over-age-in-rank for a new friendship. No one must stop making friends because he or she is past twenty, or forty, or eighty.

Have you ever seen a new family move into an established neighborhood? If the family has three small children, from three to six or seven, the kids have found new friends before the moving van is unpacked.

On the second day the six year old wants to go over

and play with his friend Johnny. His mother says who?

"You know, Mom, Johnnie who lives across the street in the brown house. He has two brothers and a sister and his dad works at home and his mom is a great cook. She gave us cookies yesterday."

Kids make friends before adults get unpacked. It might take the adults a month to meet the people beside them and across the street. Kids do this friendship routine much better than adults. Why?

They are less inhibited, less afraid.

Adults should follow their example. Someone said "The only way to make a friend is to be a friend."

Meeting new neighbors is a lot like meeting people at a party. Be open, outgoing, make eye contact and if you're new in the area, be the first to say hello.

"Hi, I'm your new neighbor Wilfred Wilbur. We just moved in yesterday. Hope the moving van didn't block your driveway."

It used to be that when a new family moved into a neighborhood, the wives all baked cookies or brownies and took over a plate full. That's a great way to meet and make a new friend. Maybe we can get the practice going again.

THE LONG ROAD TO FRIENDSHIP:

Most friends are not made instantly as they were when you were children. Adults have too many hangups to be that open and honest with strangers. Sometimes it happens, usually on a sexist basis. I've seen two women meet and in five minutes are such good friends that they would borrow each other's tooth brush.

I've also known women and men who have been slightly acquainted with each other for thirty years, but usually forget their names, don't ever visit them or socialize, who even have some of the same interests but somehow just didn't get to be good friends with them even though they lived just down the block.

A lot of people have an "attitude." This can be almost anything that slows down or stops the exchanges that are needed between two people so they can learn about each other, find mutual areas of interest and concern, be together, work together and eventually become friends.

It's a long road for most of us as we batter down one hangup after another. Friends of different races have the added hangup of racial prejudice to overcome. This is true in many parts of our country and in most large cities. This can be a devastating problem.

HOW TO DESCRIBE FRIENDSHIP:

People look at friendship in different ways. Some say it's a person you can go to with your troubles, your aches and pains, your failures and your successes and they will commiscrate or cheer with you, they will support you no matter what happens.

I like that one.

Some say a friend is somebody to give you encouragement, honest opinions, feedback, understanding, trust, respect, compassion and even a little advice.

MAKING A NEW FRIEND:

Making a new friend is a lot like building a house. It takes a lot of time. It takes work on your part. A little planning never hurts. Don't try to use a new friend before the work is all done — like trying to move into a half finished house.

Sometimes it can take a whole lifetime to make a true

friend. In times of stress a life-long friend can be made in a few minutes. Life threatening crises can bond people together so tightly in a few seconds that nothing can shake that friendship. Tragedies, accidents, disasters, and more often combat situations in wartime, can make friendships that wouldn't happen between the same two people without that special life and death bonding.

For most of us, making a friend is a matter of a lot of giving and work on our part, of more giving, of being unselfish, of being open and honest. Not everyone is capable or willing to do all of this.

Sometimes friends die for each other. Usually this isn't the intent, but it can be the result. Recently I heard of a man who rushed into a swollen river to rescue his friend and co-worker. The man trying to rescue his friend drowned, but the one originally in trouble caught a floating tree and survived.

Friendships can be gut wrenching and costly, but they're worth while. They are often all that keep some people alive when things go bad.

For most of us, the long process of making a true friend involves trust. This means we must be open and candid with our new friend, trust them with bits and pieces of the "real you" that no one else knows. Trust takes a long time to build but when it's there it is as strong or stronger than many family relationships.

Honesty with your new friend and reliability are two of the hallmarks that develop slowly and with a lot of work and concern. Even though it takes a long time for most of us to build up this trust with a new friend, it can be shattered and the person lost as a friend in one moment by violating that faith and confidence. It's a lot easier to lose a friend than it is to make one.

MAKE NEW FRIENDS:

Part of making new friends is to get yourself motivated and then go where you *have a chance* to make some new friends. If you follow the same old routine every day, chances are you'll be seeing the same people, and not exposing your experience line to new people.

Expand your scope. Attend a night class about some subject you are interested in. You've always liked photography and want your own dark room. Great! Sign up for an adult or community class that teaches photography. There usually are several of them in each community. One should be near your home.

Maybe it's weaving that interests you, or ceramics, or bowling, or ballroom dancing. Whatever it is you've always wanted to do, take a shot and sign up for it.

In this group you'll meet a lot of new people you've never even seen before. What a bunch for you to work with to form some new friendships.

This doesn't have to be a romantic relationship. You might find a same-sex person whom you can relate to, and who will remain a friend after the class is over.

You like to fish? Go on a half day fishing trip off the coast, go to a fishing lake in the mountains, hit the streams and lakes nearby with your fishing gear and be on the lookout for some new contacts. On this trip make the contacts you find more important than the fish. You could just catch a big one! (Friend that is.)

Anytime you can mix with people who have somewhat the same interests you do, you are in a prime area for making new friends. This covers church meetings, neighborhood groups, political parties, election committees, Boy Scout meetings and a thousand more.

Get active in the various groups trying to help the homeless, to help the farm workers, to increase the political awareness, to make the voter registration a much easier process.

Whatever interests you is going to interest a lot more people, and therein lies your supply of new friend candidates.

What then? use your first eight chapter hints and be open, make eye contact, say Hi first and generally be a good conversationalist. That's the foundation of any meeting with people you don't know and would like to.

Don't forget the people where you work. Try changing the time you go to lunch. You'll find a whole new crowd at the company cafeteria or in the deli across the street. Check out the next floor down or up and see if you know anyone who works there. Visit them and interact with the new folks you meet there.

Neighborhood recreation centers, condo social halls and game rooms, and apartment social rooms are prime candidates for you to use to find new people who might become new friends.

As I pointed out in the first few chapters, be open, friendly, say Hi first and use eye contact. Look around. Try to get better acquainted with people who you've been *looking around or past* everyday at work. You'll be surprised how many interesting people you can find within a hundred feet of your office.

Again, the clue is to go slow, start small. Say Hi and talk, find out more about the people, maybe hit on a shared interest in stamp collecting, or model railroads, or the ballet, or fine art on fingernails.

Don't be shy about talking and when you find someone you like, let the other person know that you're interested in something more than a quick chat. Maybe you could suggest lunch or ask him over to look at your collection of early American auto photos.

Start slow and see if there is any chance or reason why you two should not become friends. Over the months something might develop. If it doesn't, you've got a dozen more new people to talk to and perhaps interest them in being your friend.

Every suggestion made so far in this book about how to meet and greet and to get a good conversation going, applies right down the line as the best way for you to make a friend. First you meet someone, become an acquaintance, then, usually after a considerable amount of time, you can become friends.

BACK TO THE RITUAL QUESTIONS:

The information gathering questions are still a fine way to learn more about people with whom you might want to become friends. Ask what work they do. Where they're from. If they know of any good recreation centers nearby. Ask if they know of good entertainment places.

If they respond to these questions, you'll learn a lot about them quickly. You might question what part of town they live in. How long they have been at their job, how they got into that kind of work. Ask if they have a family, what their hobbies are. What they think of a current motion picture.

When you're talking with men you can always get the conversation going by saying. "What about those Lakers," or the Padres, or the Twins, or the Yankees or the Cowboys or even the heavy weight champ.

Ritual questions gain information for you about the other person. If he or she is at all interested in you, the same type of questions will be coming back at you to give the other person this same information about you.

95

REMEMBERING NAMES, DETAILS:

If this is the second or third time you've met someone who seems friendly, solidify your standing by remembering the person's name. Move on to mention something this person had been interested in or excited about the first time you talked.

"Well, Henry, haven't seen you for a few weeks. How did that vacation in Hawaii go? I see you're still a little sun tanned."

This sort of recall can do wonders. The person takes special notice of you, realizing that you remembered his name and what he was going to do for his vacation. It often is a big enough entry wedge to get a good conversation going that will result in more exchanges of information, and paving the road toward friendship with another square or two of tile.

How do you remember names? Look back at the chapter on names and you'll find half a dozen crutches to help you recall a name. It isn't easy, but it's vital in today's business and social world. Don't count on the hostess providing name tags. Most won't, and those tags that get used often can't be read anyway. Remember those names.

WHEN TO GIVE YOUR NAME:

Some people worry about when they should use their name in a social/business situation. I like it right out front.

"Hi, I'm Joe Johnson with Johnson Electronics. I've been looking forward to meeting you."

That way it's there and you're on record and no hiding behind badges or silence. If the other person is even half human, he or she will respond with a name and firm if that's important, and you have the start of a conversation going.

Others I've known will move around and talk, but they will give their name only if they think they have found someone they would like to know better, can trust, or who will be a benefit to their careers.

"Hello, I'm Mary Jo Whipperville. I met you a year ago at the Atlanta Convention. How is that new line of mini computers coming along for you?"

This is admittedly a bit self centered and conservative, but many women are reluctant to go glad handing around a meeting or social function spreading their name to anyone who will listen. There is a time to be conservative and watchful, but don't overdo it.

When most people hold out their hand and give their name, they expect you to respond in like fashion. Almost everyone will. Friendliness is catching and that's what I'm trying to get across here.

If there is a man in the group you definitely don't want to meet, do your best to avoid him. If you get trapped where there is an introduction, be your coolest self, be civil, shake his hand and exchange names, then quickly excuse yourself and end the conversation at once.

Some men come on too strong too quickly. This is especially true when they meet an attractive woman for the first time. The rule here is to take it slow and easy. She's a knockout? Good. You're no slouch yourself. Don't oversell. Don't be pushy. Be casual and informal and keep everything comfortable.

Maybe the third time you talk to the lady, you might indicate that you'd like to meet her again, for a cup of coffee or lunch sometime.

"I'd like that," is a great answer to your invitation.

"I'm not sure of my schedule, but the next two weeks are filled with this convention coming up." An answer like this is enough of a put off to make you thank her and turn away. You can't win every time.

WORK AT FRIENDSHIP:

Let's say at the garden club you meet a new couple about your age you and your wife hit it off with them. They are nuts about epihiliums the same way you are. It's blooming season, so invite them over to see your new beauties now in flower.

If the evening goes well, you can expect a return invitation. If none comes after a month or two, ask them back for cards or dessert or just to look around your potting shed. Don't let the chance for an extended friendship wither on the potting shed floor.

Perhaps the other couple has a small place not suited for entertaining. Tell them that's no problem, they can come to your home and bring a dessert. Suggest you pick them up in your car for the next garden club meeting.

Offer to take them to the county fair where there is a huge flower display.

Go out of your way to be friendly with them if you feel this is a couple who might fit well into your group of friends. After several meetings, invite them to a larger gathering at your house so they can get to know your other friends.

Building friendships is done with one small brick at a time. It takes a lot of them to make a sidewalk through your garden, and even more to build a new brick house.

BUILDING FRIENDSHIP WITH COMPLIMENTS:

Compliments are the miser's bouquet of roses. They cost nothing to give, can work wonders, and never fade or grow limp and get thrown away. A fine compliment can last for years.

In your conversations, don't forget to drop a few compliments from time to time. Make them sincere and don't make it habit to spew them out like business cards. A true compliment can make a person's whole evening a success.

"My, but I like that combination of sweater, skirt and blouse. It looks just wonderful on you."

A compliment like this from one person to another, male or female, can be a thoughtful way of showing approval and boosting a person's self confidence. Remember the compliment, most of us forget this too often. If we're not worried about how WE LOOK, or about WHAT WE'RE GOING TO SAY, or about HOW TO IMPRESS SOMEONE, chances are we'll be able to observe the other person and when we feel like making a compliment, we will do it.

You have to mean it when you give a compliment. Don't say it in a flat, routine way. Get some emotion into your voice and manner. Then the person will understand.

Remember when Sally Fields accepted her Oscar for best acting award and broke down. "You *really* like me!" she said to her fellow actors and it was on camera for a nation wide TV audience to hear. Sincerity is the key here.

SEND A NOTE:

Note paper and stamps are one of the best ways to further a friendship. If you've been to a party and enjoyed yourself, sit down the next day and send a quick little thank you note to your hostess. Not one in fifty people ever do this.

If you meet someone at a social or business function and enjoyed talking with them and perhaps picked up some important points in the business that you didn't know, sit down the next day and send a quick little note of appreciation to whomever it was who taught, encouraged or inspired you.

The written word is powerful. It shows the other person that you took the time to sit down and write a note, found the right address and sent it on its way. What you say isn't so important as the simple ACT of sending the message.

Such small, friendly gestures have cemented and continued many a nebulous acquaintance into a firm friend.

So, what does it all add up to? If you want to make a new friend, be a friend yourself. That's the basic. Then practice all of the good conversation techniques talked about previously. Be honest and giving and make an effort to be a friend of others.

Now let's look at a little different aspect of conversation. One of the things a lot of us wonder about and worry about is flirting. You've seen people do it with great results. The problem is just how can YOU flirt and have it be productive and not destructive? How? turn the page and read on.

10

HOW TO FLIRT. . .SAFELY

Flirting has developed a bad name lately, especially these days with all the hoopla about sexual harassment. The whole harassment thing has been blown out of proportion. True there is some of that out there, but there are a lot more people who are wanting and wishing for some friends and companions and dates.

Flirting should be fun, casual, entertaining, a way to brighten up your day and in no way should lead down any path you don't want it to. Flirting itself is harmless, as long as you stay in control of the situation. If it's starting to go too far, put the brakes on at once and move on to another person or group.

One of my friends says that flirty isn't difficult at all. The most important element of flirting we've been talking about all through this book, that's simply meeting people in an open and gracious way and being *friendly*.

Being friendly is flirting? Not the whole thing of course, but it's the basic, the underlying element. You can't flirt if you're a grouch or mad or annoyed, or upset, or just waiting to get out of the place. It's the wrong mood, the wrong tone, the wrong approach.

The first thing to remember is that being warm and friendly is the underlying groundwork for all flirting.

101

Flirting is being friendly and friendly is the way to start. Remember that most people will react to you and treat you the way you treat them. If you bark at them and snarl and frown, chances are you'll get the same tone and attitude right back at you.

The same thing applies with friendly flirting. If the other person is at all receptive to your flirting, he or she will soon be flirting right back at you. Don't expect anything else. You have to open the door and start the friendly flirting, or you won't get to first base even being a friend.

SOME BASIC TRAINING:

You don't have to be the most handsome hunk in town or the best looking woman in the county to be great at flirting. One thing you do need to do is to *want to flirt*. Some people equate flirting with that one step beyond being open and friendly so you can let others know that you're looking for a romantic relationship.

There's nothing wrong with that definition at all. To let others know, you flirt a little and if it helps you to get that step beyond the introductions and polite conversation, so much the better.

To be a good flirt you don't have to be rich or have a smooth line of chatter, or swing your hips or bat your eyelashes. Just wanting to is your first basic training step.

The next step is to check out the field. Know when you can or should flirt and when not to. If the biggest jerk in town is in your group, you know you don't want to flirt with him. Use your best judgement about when to flirt. A funeral would be a bad flirting time, but a wedding is a great time to flirt.

Pick out a likely candidate and if possible check him out with other women in the group. Is he a flake? Does he have a job or is he a gigolo? Has anyone gone out with him?

Beyond that, use your common sense and your flirt meter. How does he register as a potential flirt candidate? Remember here the basic conversational tool: always treat others the way you would like to be treated yourself. This applies doubly to flirting.

Flirting can be a slow process. Take your time, be patient. You talk with this woman for a half hour and offer all sorts of flirtatious overtures, but she simply doesn't connect with them. Maybe she's having a bad day, or just got fired, or her best friend died.

Don't rush her. If she's worth taking out, she's worth waiting for. Find out if she'll be back at that spot, and show up again and make the second effort. Most of us like to think we're not easy, we're worth waiting for. The slower the flirtation, the more lasting the relationship might be. In any event, something that is slow in coming is often much more satisfying and memorable than the quick flirt, date and parting that so often happens these days.

Stay ready to flirt at any time. Some of the best flirting opportunities sneak up on you. The woman who goes to the grocery store in a bandanna and curlers, no makeup, and in sweats, might be passing up a great opportunity. She might run into a hunk or a genius in the frozen food section.

Single men spend a lot of time in the frozen food section because the prepared meals are so easy to heat and eat. A great place to meet men.

The idea is that the more ready you are to meet and greet and flirt, anywhere you are, the better your chances of finding that Mr. or Miss Wonderful.

Men have the same problem when they rush out to the store in their clogs, no socks, old jeans and sweat shirt and without having shaved for two days and hair in a tangled

103

mop. Not a good platform for launching those flirting missiles.

Be ready, physically and emotionally. When you go out of your apartment, leave behind all of your doubts, your failures, your first and second marriages, and those unproductive nights of cruising the singles bars finding only half loaded men and women who were more interested in their drinks than anything else.

LIST YOUR FLIRTING GOALS:

It's always good on any new campaign to make a list of what you want. Same with flirting. Put down a list of what you hope to get out of some casual flirting.

• Meet new, interesting people.
• Get out of the old rut.
• Meet men or women other than those at the office.
• It can make you feel more alive, more human and worth something.
• To meet someone compatible so you won't be lonely.
• To learn to be more at ease and natural with the opposite sex.
• So you won't have to eat alone at a cafe or restaurant.

So what do you want from your flirting? Is it short term friendships, so you won't be lonesome, or a longer deeper relationship?

Most people think of flirting in a narrow sense. They say that men flirt so they can get as many women into their beds as possible. They say that women flirt primarily to find someone to marry them.

There's some truth in both statements, but on the broad range of singles today, there is a lot less of both in reality than there used to be. Men and women are looking for relationships. It's easy to pick out the man on the make strictly for a night in bed. It's just as easy to ignore him.

The woman with only marriage in mind is not so easy to spot at once, but after a date or two it's much more obvious.

HOW TO FLIRT:

A lot of us have been mildly flirting for years and probably didn't even realize it. When you consciously try to flirt, it may be a little harder, but hang in there and try a few times and a few ways and look for those small victories that we all need. You'll see results and progress. Here are some of the tired and true ways to flirt – politely.

• *Say hello with a flair!* Get some energy into your voice, some sparkle. Make whoever you're talking to believe he's the most important person in the world to you. Have you ever talked to a tape recorder? Try saying hello to your tape recorder. Say it twenty times and play it back to see how you sound.

Would you enjoy talking to you when you say hello that way? Practice putting some tingle, some excitement in your voice. Practice it again and again. Get your "Hello," or your "Hi there, it's good to meet you." Practice it until you're sure you can say an exciting and interesting greeting. It will pay off.

• *Always use your great smile.* You're not sure of your smile? Go in the bathroom right now and practice that smile. The sincere, warm believable smile. Nothing phoney or leering. Just a good open mouth smile that shows some teeth, puts a little crinkle at the corners of your eyes and is honest and the real you.

You may need to practice this one several times. Be sure you can use that "great" smile anytime you want to. It's a good idea to practice your hello at the same time you're working on your smile.

• *Offer to shake hands first.* If you're not a Hollywood

type, shaking hands is the best way to greet a stranger. Too formal for flirting? Not on your life. A handshake can tell a lot about a person. Is it firm and polite? Is it relaxed and casual? Shaking hands is your first touch with this person. Holding the others hand, squeezing it then letting go are all sensual contacts.

• *Always make eye contact.* Nothing unusual here. This is flirting? It can be. It's the first part of any friendly meeting. By concentrating on a person's eyes you can convey much more than a simple look. You can imply all sorts of wonderful things, and it doesn't take a Sherlock Holmes to pick up on the eye to eye signals.

Eye contact can be made with someone half way across the room. If it works, it works. Always make eye contact when you meet someone.

• *Use the person's name.* Repeat the person's name three times in your meeting. Say it when you first are introduced, and again a few minutes later. Always use the person's name when you say good bye.

Our names are important to us. We all like to hear our name, and by remembering it, you are saying that this person is important enough to you that you will remember the name.

• *Ask your new friend's life story.* We all like to talk about ourselves. Keep asking your friend about his early life, dig into his life story, his schooling, his career, what his secret desire is. Keep him or her talking about themselves. Is this flirting? It's a way to keep the other person interested in you. That's the name of the flirting game.

• *Toy with hair or clothing.* Rhythmic, repetitive actions somehow are sexy and comforting. Women can toy with their hair, dangle a shoe and rock it back and forth, play with an ear ring, twist a ring on your finger.

Men can adjust a tie, play with cuff links, swirl a drink, comb your hair, bounce a ball or flip a coin. All of these can set up some kind of chemistry between people.

- *Whisper to her!* There is something secret and hidden and intimate and sexy about whispering. You have to get your body close to the other person. Your face close to hers. A whisper makes the other person feel selected, chosen, special. You're excluding all others and telling just her or him. That's a fine way of flirting that produces instant reactions.
- *Flirt, backoff, flirt.* Make your first pitch the strongest, your flirting outrageous, compelling, productive. Then after a few minutes after you have the intended's attention, back off. Go to the bathroom, go get a drink, talk to someone else a moment.

You're deliberately delaying your return to the person you were flirting with. They will wonder what's the matter? You had been talking to her, flirting, coming on, now you're cool and detached and not even right beside her.

Come back and bring that drink, or apologize for being gone and gear up the flirting again. Whisper something you just heard across the room. Toy with your hair and ask her some interesting question about her early life. Move back into flirting, but not as strong as you did before. It lets the other person know you're still interested and gives them the idea that you can still be lost. Many people will try hard to get something they think is slipping away from them or is almost lost.

- *On a second meeting with that special someone, bring a small gift.* Something thoughtful but not expensive: a wild kind of cheese, a magazine, a funny card, a funny household gadget, something for his car or her office. A spur of the moment trinket that can be given and forgotten.
- *Show a personal concern.* If the person you're interested in tucks in a sweater, ask her if she's cold and move her out of a draft. If his glass is empty, ask if you can go bring him a fresh drink. If a person looks tired, ask if you can find them a chair.

Try to think of anything that this person might want or need. Pretend that you're a servant in the house and your only duties are to keep the person happy and warm and satisfied. Much the way that a flight attendant does on an airliner. This shows concern, nurturing, caring about the person as a person, and not just as a pretty face or a hunk.

• *Use the power of the human touch.* Touching is the most intimate of the ways of flirting. You've seen lovers who simply can't keep their hands off each other even in public. There are hugs and cuddling and kissing and arms around waists and sitting on laps. Fine for lovers, not for flirting.

The flirting touch is tender, sensitive, casual, brief. You might brush lint off a man's jacket sleeve. A man might gently brush long golden hair from a woman's eyes.

You must not touch anyone in a way or a place where there could be any sexual overtones.

A woman might touch a man's shoulder and then point to something in a silent signal. The silly child's game of finger walking can be enchanting. Four or five steps up an arm with fingers is enough. It's amusing, sexy, complicated.

The broken sentence touch is also effective. "I don't know, John," (pause as she brushes lint off his sleeve) if I should go out with you or not."

The words mean one thing, the touch something else. Touching briefly, tenderly, thoughtfully, can lead to longer touches later in your relationship that will be much more exciting.

• *Use flirting props.* Think of the number of things you can leave at someone's apartment so you need to go back and get them: gloves, briefcase, sunglasses, umbrella, appointment book. If it's an umbrella, think how close you'll need to get to have two of you under that one little bumbershoot.

Sunglasses are especially effective. Taking them off for a comment and putting them back on turns on and off the other persons eye contact with you. That lets you play with the glasses and use them to mask certain reactions or drop them and show him you're serious. Great props.

Other flirting props include a mirror, a car, even something you've made or written yourself. Flowers are a hard one. Men, for a first date you might try one bloom, not a bouquet. Most men are embarrassed if a woman brings a man even one flower.

Aspirin? Yes, aspirin. You can fake a headache and go up to this gorgeous blonde or the hunk and say you have a pounding headache and ask if they have any kind of pain pills. Works wonders. Right away that someone is trying to take care of you. The rest is up to friendly flirting.

The end result of all of this flirting might be for you to get an honest to goodness, bonafide, respectable date. Speaking of dates, that's what we'll be speaking of in the next chapter, so please turn the page and continue.

11

HOW TO FIND A DATE

All right, I finally got down to it, true? The whole idea here of meeting people and making friends is with the fond hope that one of those new friends will ask you for a date — even just a cup of coffee or a lunch. At least to start.

Here are some of the best methods and reasons and ways and places to find a date that you've ever come across. Take out your notebook and jot them down for full time, on-person, use. Never leave the house without them.

LET'S MAKE A LIST:

You probably already have a list, a long sheet of paper showing exactly what you want in a date. First what kind of a list is it, a Cadillac type or a Volkswagen style?

Your Caddy list probably looks like this:

- At least six feet tall.
- Dark brown hair with reddish tints.
- A winning personality.
- Not more than thirty-five.
- Must be involved in ballet and the library committee.
- An expert on jumping horses.
- Must work to help the homeless.

• Be a member of Greenpeace.
• Be a Democrat.

That's your Cadillac list, your wish-you-could-find-one. You know you can't find that man. So you start working on your Volkswagen list, the practical one.

Volkswagen list:
• Someone who respects me as a person.
• A non-smoker and non-drinker.
• A person easy to talk to who will be a good listener.
• Someone who will not be afraid to make a long term commitment if we get that far.

Hey, now we're getting somewhere. That's your bottom line list. Anything else from the top list will be helpful, but not essential.

Yes, your list will change from time to time. Especially your wish list is going to change as you do. But your basic needs won't be all that different from one year to the next.

Now, you know generally what kind of a companion you're looking for, just how do you find him or her with things the way they are today?

LOCATE PLACES YOU ARE COMFORTABLE GOING TO:

If you're just getting into this "looking for a date" routine, you don't have to do it alone. Search your friends and find another person in your same single, unattached state and strike a bargain. You'll both go date hunting together.

Say there's a neighborhood bar nearby that has a small dance floor and a friendly crowd. Go with your friend and as soon as you get in the door split up. Two women together or two men together can give the wrong impression and make it ten times harder to strike up a conversation.

Arrange to meet from time to time in the restroom to compare notes.

The first twenty minutes will be the hardest. You'll be mad at yourself for coming, you'll feel alone and think people are talking about you. But you paid for your drink so you might as well stick it out until you finish it.

That's a good sign. Don't be desperate, be yourself. You might even have a good time. You might meet someone to talk to, or dance with. At least you're out in the mainstream and watching for someone you'll enjoy talking with.

It doesn't have to be a bar. Your choice might be a church bingo game, a dog show, a literary tea, a poetry reading, a political action committee, a save the whales campaign.

Wherever it is, be yourself, enjoy the affair, be open and smile and say hi first and meet everyone you can. Oh, yes, keep watching for that person you want to get to know better.

Parties? Sure, you can go to parties alone whether you're a man or a woman. Parties are not couple affairs. Whether it's a wedding reception, a holiday party, or just a get acquainted time for some new people on the block, go and mix and use all of the helps in this book for meeting people, and you will. Parties are for having fun, so don't make it a chore. Have fun yourself and you'll find someone who wants to share your fun.

BE RELAXED, DON'T PRESS SO HARD:

Them who has, gets. True. When you have a relationship going you probably meet a dozen or so people you could really hit it off with. Now that you're alone you can't find a one of that dozen. Curious?

It could be because you're pressing too hard. Success likes success. When you're with somebody, you tend to be more relaxed, more casual, more open and friendly than when you've been dumped for some cheap blonde. When you're open and friendly you attract other people who are the same way and it's easy to get acquainted.

Now that your old man has moved on to a new squeeze, you think you're fat, and your clothes don't fit right and your make up is wrong and you need a new hair style and your shoes...ugg!

Stop it already. Now more than ever you need to slow down on the worry, to stop the self criticism. Now you need to concentrate on being open, friendly, to smile, to go to parties with the idea that you're going to enjoy yourself no matter what happens.

With that kind of an attitude, you'll do a whole lot better, you'll meet new people and make friends, and maybe even get a date for lunch....or make one. So relax, don't take yourself so seriously. Have fun, and fun will find you.

BE A HELLO PERSON:

Several times in this book I've suggested that you be the first to say "Hi,". This is simply good and friendly practice. If you tend to tie up with strangers and have trouble walking up to a man or a woman who is appealing to you and saying that first Hi, then what you need is practice.

Make it a point to say hello to most of the people you meet. In a small town it seems that when you walk down Main Street half the people say hello even if they don't know each other.

This would be surprising in the middle of New York City or Chicago or Los Angeles or San Diego. But it isn't unusual in a business or a hallway or an apartment complex or a condo. Get used to saying that hello to the mailman, the grocery store clerk, the motorman, the janitor, the secretaries and the people in the gym.

The more that you can say hello to strangers, the easier

it will be for you to say that vital first hello to that knockout in the miniskirt and the short red hair who just came to the party alone. Zowwwwwwwie! Get on your shanks mares and amble over there and use all of that new found confidence and be the first to say hello. If you don't there will be a dozen guys darting her way.

Saying hello and Hi, should be a friendly way of life for you. Every day, in all social situations and many casual meetings in the hall and cafeteria and at parties. Do it, you'll find you meet more interesting folks that way.

LEARN A FEW GOOD JOKES TO TELL:

The Lone Ranger of Western Fame and his loyal Indian friend Tonto were in a race against some marauding Cheyenne. At last they rode up to the top of a steep hill where they could defend themselves. They looked out and saw five thousand Indians on one side.

Tonto looked on the other side and saw five thousand more Indians. The Lone Ranger took off his mask and wiped his forehead. He reached out his hand to shake with Tonto.

"Old friend, it looks like we're really in trouble this time. With ten thousand Indians out there I don't see how we can possibly escape."

Tonto pulled back his hand and shook his head. He pulled off his shirt and grabbed his bow and arrows. Then he looked at the Lone Ranger.

"What do you mean *we're in trouble*, white man!"

Learn a few clean jokes or stories you can tell. They are an ideal way to break the ice in a group or with an individual. Often this will start a round of jokes as everyone wants to get on the entertainment committee.

You don't have any good experiences? Borrow some or tell what happened to someone else.

Tell a joke or a story. It could be the start of something great — for you.

STUDY THE SINGLES PUBLICATIONS:

In most cities of any size, there are publications, aimed at singles. These might be tabloids that come out monthly, or sections of magazines or daily newspapers.

Most newspapers have a "singles" column written by a local single person who highlights activities especially slanted to the single person.

In these publications you'll find dozens of advertisements for singles activities, club news, notes about happenings, news stories.

You'll often find notices of special meetings of singles such as Parents Without Partners, and dozens of sports activities and game nights in halls from churches to the YWCA to the local political clubs.

Snip out the activities that appeal to you. There usually are so many that you couldn't possibly go to all of them in one week. By posting these activities on your "ACTION" bulletin board, you'll have a continuing selection of things to do on week ends or on Wednesday nights or Sunday afternoons.

Get your hands on every singles publication, newsletter and activity roster that you can find, and then utilize them and find events that you'll feel at home in and where you can enjoy yourself. Remember, the more fun you have, the more fun others will have and the more attractive you'll be.

UPSCALE CLOTHING STORES:

Now this one might sound sneaky and it is, but only just a little. Give it a try just for fun. If it doesn't work, what have you lost.

The next time you're near a good men's store, and you're female, stop in and browse around. Tell any clerk who approaches you that you're looking for exactly the right present for your boyfriend. Browse the clothes, but also watch for men shoppers.

Say you spot this interesting man about your age who is nicely dressed and looking at sweaters. Walk over and check out the sweaters and wait for him to look at you. You made sure he doesn't have a wedding ring.

"Excuse me, but I'm kind of lost in here. I'm looking for a sweater for my brother. He's about your size, is that medium or large he'd need?"

"I wear a large, but if he's over six-two or so he might need an extra large."

"Which color do you like, the brown one or the green? I'm not good on men's clothes at all."

"You're probably asking the wrong person. If it were me I'd like that shade of brown best."

From there it's up to you.

The same thing works in women's stores, even better. Stay away from the lingerie section, too many men get too embarrassed to get their mouths open.

Try the sweaters or jackets, maybe blouses, and try the same routine about buying a gift. Size and style are always good questions.

The busier the store the better. That means more shoppers and more prospects to chose from. On a real busy day at a clothing store, it's almost like Christmas....for you with all of those pretty, interesting people.

116

TRY BOOKSTORES, LIBRARIES, VIDEO STORES:

Bookstores are the best places to browse and spend some time. They also are a good spot to meet someone with interests like your own. Is your thing Western novels? Most bookstores and used bookstores have racks and racks of Westerns and western history.

Enjoy yourself at the shelves and keep an eye out for someone you might want to talk to. You'll be surprised how many women read Western novels.

If your interest is in mainstream novels, or in the self help area, you'll find others in those sections diligently checking for books.

When you find someone who might be fun to talk to you might use the "who wrote it" angle.

"Miss, I'm sorry to bother you but these books are listed by author and I'm trying to find that self help book called, *Never say Die*. Do you remember who wrote it?"

"Oh, Hi. Yes, I saw it here somewhere just a minute ago. I've only been through to the E's so it can't be far. Yes, here it is. Caldwell wrote it."

"Thanks, you're a good book finder. Not one of my talents. I like to read them, but finding them is harder."

And away you go.

Libraries are a bit more quiet, but a soft word or two can get across the idea, and that broad shouldered young man with the dimples might help you find a book you want. Just be sure it's a real book so he won't suspect.

These kind of stores are ideal for meeting someone who have something of the same interests that you do...

SINGLES RUSH HOUR AT THE GROCERY:

The grocery store and supermarket are still one of the best spots to find eligible partners. At last report all singles must still eat three times a day...well at least twice a day. Most of them need to buy a few groceries, and light bulbs and toothpaste.

Do your grocery shopping after work or on Saturday. Those are the big singles rush hours for food stores. One of the favorite spots for men and women alike is the frozen food aisle. The packaged dinners and pizzas and even microwave cakes and pop in the oven and bake pies, draw singles like a hunger pang.

This aisle is heaven for quick cook meals for singles. Hit the frozen dinner section and ask the blonde without rings and the cute little behind and big smile if she's ever tried this brand.

"The Swanson dinners, are they as good as they look?"

The blonde giggled. "Hey, I'm not sure. I'm not really into cooking, but I can do frozen dinners in the microwave. I always go for the turkey."

She looked up, soft blue eyes interested. "Do you like turkey frozen dinners?"

"I do, but I just bought this frozen chicken banquette dinner for two. Would you like to share it with me tonight?"

Zowie, Zap and Bang!

Who knows, the supermarket might become the haven for the singles. I heard of one supermarket who's manager invited all singles to come shopping on a certain evening of the week. They had special singles prices, and punch and cookies and a sign up for a bus trip. They made quite a promotion. It brought in a lot of singles and after the promotion was over, the singles kept going back to that store to meet their friends, and to get better acquainted.

It was a natural spot for inviting someone to a dinner — that they had just bought.

OUT OF TOWN:

As a single have you ever been out of town for a few days and spent them in a hotel room? Lonely wasn't it. Remember how you worked at doing something every night? You went to a movie, or to a Broadway play or the ballet or an opera. The point is that you *worked at finding something to do.*

Hold that thought. Now you're home but you can still *pretend that you are out of town.* Check the newspaper. What plays are on, what movies, what activities? Most newspapers have a section on things to do this week or this week end. Clip it out and save it.

In San Diego, for example, one week there were 27 different live performance plays that you could go to. Most of them were little theatre groups, but they do surprisingly good work.

So this week, pretend that you are out of town, and actively hunt for something wild, interesting, strange, unusual, and fun to do. It will perk up your whole week, and while you're at it, be open, friendly, make eye contact and say Hi first. That's the way to meet a friend, find a date, maybe strike up that long lasting relationship.

PAR FOR THE COURSE: REJECTIONS.

Hey, nobody is perfect. Nobody wins all the time. Remember this when you walk up to that big guy at the party who has been watching you. You smile and say hi and introduce yourself, and he ignores your hand and slips past you and heads for the bar. Just because he didn't smile back and talk to you for half an hour is no sign that you were at fault. You just weren't his type. Maybe he was near sighted and couldn't even see you standing over there.

So, don't go down in flames. Grin, get another glass of punch and watch for a new candidate for a friend. You're not selling stocks and bonds here or even life insurance, you're out for a good time and that won't happen if you let one failure to communicate get to you.

Remember that not everyone you meet at a party or a gathering will be right for you and some of them will be so wrong you'll know it at once.

The trouble is, you can't know if that person is right or wrong for you before you meet them and try to get to know them. When you find out, move on.

If the score card shows that you have met five dumbos in a row, it doesn't mean that you are the one at fault. It's called the law of probability, and no way is it even handed. Just keep on pitching that beautiful smile of yours and that form fitting dress and your cheerful hello and good conversation and you're going to have a run of good luck.

PUTTING THEM ALL TOGETHER:

How to get a date is a big topic and whole books have been written on it. The important elements are to be sure that you're ready, that you've done your home work on your hello and on your smile. Know that your self confidence is high and that you're ready to launch yourself on an adventure to find a date as well as to have a good time.

Then search out the places where you feel at home and where there are people with your same interests. The key words here are to be natural and have fun. Others like to be with people who are enjoying themselves.

Don't take failures to heart. Put them down as the other

person's loss and move on to better pickings.

If you're relaxed and enjoying yourself, you'll soon meet someone who likes the real you and wants to be with you. Never give up. And.....smile.

We didn't touch on it in this chapter, but some people get anxious when they meet strangers. That shouldn't be a problem. I'm going to offer you some suggestions about anxiety. To find out, move on to the next chapter.....right now.

12

REDUCING YOUR ANXIETY

Anxiety. Most of us from time to time have experienced some painful uneasiness over a coming event. That's simple anxiety. Some people say they have a sense of apprehension and fear. They sweat, their pulse races and their muscles tense. Many times anxiety can send a person racing for the bathroom.

People react in different ways. Some people simply sit and stare, not able to talk normally or react until the time of tension is past.

For most of us, we get a little nervous and jittery and we sweat a little and we wish we were somewhere else, anywhere else.

Self doubt is one of the biggest causes of anxiety. Look at the old pro football player just before a game. He might lie down and have a short nap. The rookie is pacing up and down the locker room pounding his helmet, chewing on his mouth piece, yelling at his team mates. You can bet he's nervous and upset and he's sweating already and his heart is racing a mile a second.

The old pro hears the cleats hit the concrete runway. He gets up, stretches, puts on his helmet and wanders out to the playing field. That afternoon he turns in a pro-bowl quality performance. The rookie missed two tackles, made four and finally in the fourth quarter lost his anxiety and his nervousness and played the way the pro scouts knew he could.

DID I ACT THE FOOL OUT THERE?

If you've ever asked your date or your mate this question after a meeting or a party, it shows that you really have a lot of self doubts brought on by anxiety. Almost everyone I know gets nervous when they must get up before a group and speak, or give a report, or even give their opinion. These people are not used to doing this, it's new and strange and everyone is looking at them and they know they've never been any good at public speaking.

Anxiety jumps up and grabs them, and sure enough, what they had to say, and had learned word for word, just can't get out through all of the tension.

When I bought my first new car I was so nervous and up tight that I could hardy bargain with the salesman. I kept laughing. There wasn't anything to laugh about.

"Yes, I do like the color of this car," I'd say and I'd laugh.

The salesman showed me the engine and the new way it was positioned and I thought of the price sticker I'd seen on the window and I laughed.

My wife kept looking at me wondering what was going on. The salesman brought out the trade in allowance figure on my old car and I looked at the amount in surprise and I laughed. I really broke up when he showed me the total cost of the car, taxes, insurance and expected downpayment.

All of my laughing was my way right then of trying to relieve the tension, break down the anxiety, slow down my pulse and stop my sweating. I didn't know why at the time I was laughing so much. I was excited about buying a car, but anxious? Not a chance. I used to write sales training for car salesmen. I knew all the tricks, all the ways to cut down the price, how to leave the salesman gasping.

I was so nervous I forgot them all. Sure, I bought the car, and my wife asked me what was so funny. I didn't even realize that I had been laughing up a storm.

CAN A GROWN MAN EVER CRY?

We've all seen people laugh in tense and tragic circumstances. After funerals at the survivor's home the gathering often is jovial and sometimes boisterous even without any alcohol around.

Some people would rather laugh than cry. They reverse the emotions to conceal what they feel deep down inside. They say it's always better to laugh than it is to cry.

Sometimes it is, but there certainly is plenty of room for most people, men and women, to cry.

I was in Detroit, Michigan where I had moved to a new job. My wife and small son were set to come out the next day. I had been there for three weeks and missed them both terribly. The night before they were to leave, I called them, and my wife said that they couldn't get out of the airport.

It was fogged in at Portland, Oregon, and nothing was moving. They would be at least two days late. We talked a little more and when I hung up the phone — I cried. I had never felt so lonely or sad or dumped upon in my life. Oh, they came two days later and by then I had recovered. There are plenty of times to cry.

In the business world, it's tougher. Most men and women alike never want to be seen crying at work. If the boss chews you out and you break down and cry, it's usually a small mark against you. Some particularly abusive boss might try later to make you cry again for his own enjoyment, to prove how powerful he is.

Most people in business try to maintain their composure in emotional situations, to hold it in as long as they can. When possible they retreat to the bathroom or an empty office and have their cry.

Crying is often a release and the person feels much better after it's over.

Just as some people laugh at tragic events, others find that they are so emotionally moved at a particularly joyful event that they cry. Women traditionally cry at weddings. I've never figured out on that one if they're happy or sad. I'll leave that one up to the psychiatrists.

Crying tears of joy is a term that is often heard. Our emotions are powerful and should not be held inside. A good cry, a fine laugh, an outburst of anger from time to time can do a lot for most people to let off steam or anger or to express joy and keep us on an even keel.

RATIONAL THINKING:

Many people believe that through rational thought we can learn to think more discriminatively. In this way, they can improve their ability to form and control their emotions. This way they can accept their limitations and stop torturing themselves about reaching impossible goals.

Rational thinking can mean that a person can block out a lot of negative emotions that can have a bad effect on his life. By simply going around them, the way is much more clear and positive.

With this idea, anxiety doesn't have a chance. Now you can be a rational thinker and eliminate the negatives, and you can take a long hard look at the real stresses in your life and figure out how to eliminate or reduce them.

Someone defined rational thinking as: "The way of thinking which is life preserving and enables a person to pursue self-defined goals with a minimum of unwanted conflicts."

DEFUSING ANXIETY:

Have you ever watched a pole vaulter at a big meet, or a high jumper, or even a basketball free throw shooter get ready to perform? Most of them have little nervous habits they do, but many will stop and without moving take two or three deep breaths.

What does that do? Try it. For most of us, a deep breath relaxes us, lets us get in the best possible physical and mental state before the last try at twenty feet in the Olympics, say.

Some people believe that by holding your breath for a slow count to three seconds, letting out the air and holding your breath again for three seconds, you can relax yourself. If you do this three times, it's supposed to melt away your nervousness and anxiety like magic. Try it. If it works for you, use it.

Those nine seconds are going to give you time enough to do some high powered thinking as well.

Let's say you're going to the big boss's office for your yearly job evaluation. Hey, this is tough stuff. If you don't measure up, if you aren't doing better this year than you did last year, you might not even have a job, let alone that raise you were hoping for.

Now this is anxiety time!

Try the breathing routine as you wait outside for your appointment. If you're just as wired when you get into the hard chair in the big boss's office, try something else.

Look your boss right in the eye. "Mr. Jones, I don't know why, but I'm as anxious as a long tailed cat in a room full of rocking chairs."

Just saying that you are anxious does miracles for most

people. It helps reduce their worry, lets them settle down a little, maybe even relax. If your boss gives a little chuckle about visualizing this long tailed cat and ten rocking chairs rolling back and forth, it will help you relax even more.

Hard questions? I've seen witnesses on the stand take a big breath after they get asked a tough question. It gives them a moment more to think, and it also might help them to relax a little bit as well.

In a non court room situation, the old ploy of repeating a question is always good.

"Okay, Pete, where did you hide the secret code?"

"You want to know where I hid the secret code?"

See how much time you've earned for yourself already? He answers your question and by then you've had your three breaths, come up with a solid lie about the code book, and have stalled long enough for the good guys to break in and rescue you.

ANGER PRODUCES ANXIETY:

With most of us, anger can be a major producer of a dozens of different kinds of anxiety. We get mad and we start sweating and our blood races and all at once we're in a fine state of a major upset.

Many times this anger on a person to person basis is when we figure somebody has wronged us, the boss has dumped on us again, or the whole world is against us.

One thing about anger, if it is left bottled up in that steam cooker of yours, it can blow your ears right off your head. It's best to get the anger out in the open. If your gripe is with another worker or a friend, spit it out, right now before it can grow and fester.

"Hey, Tyler. What do you mean I'm not good enough to work through that next series of blueprints? I can read a print as well as you can."

(So here you have verbalized what you considered an insult and a slight by your co worker. It's out there for him to hear and understand.)

"Joe," Tyler said. "I really don't think I said you weren't good enough to work the next series. I wanted Bill to do it so that would leave you free to come with me up to the Chief Engineer's office and tell him about the problem we found in the specs in the electrical on number three engine."

(Joe had completely misread his being left out on the blueprint work. He misinterpreted what Tyler said. By getting it out in the open quickly, everyone is turned around, the anger is washed away since it was uncalled for, and everyone is happy.)

True, as it says on a TV commercial, happy endings are easy on TV and in a book like this. They aren't always so easy in real life. But by trying to get your anger out, confronting the one you figure wronged you, the whole thing can be worked out quickly and you can dump off that load of anxiety and get on with your life.

Rational thought processes and a quick "airing" of your anger are both good ways to take care of your anxiety.

Another is to establish a strong self image and project it. When others feel that you're confident, they often try to match your confidence and the whole "tone" and feeling in a workplace or in a relationship can mellow and blossom and grow.

I started my work life as a newspaper reporter. I'd never intended to do that tough job. I fully expected to go through journalism school and come out and be a famous, rich and pampered great American novelist.

Didn't work out that way, so I got a job on a newspaper, a weekly, then a small daily and I learned a lot. But the first year or so I really didn't like calling up someone and getting a story. I hated to go downtown and walk into a strange office and interview someone I'd never met before.

I did it, that was my job, but I was never comfortable with it. It wasn't until a lot of years later, that I suddenly realized that I wasn't afraid of anybody anymore. I could walk up to the mayor and say howdy or criticize him. I could get to my feet and speak my viewpoint and not collapse. I could travel coast to coast and not even worry about it. I could talk with anybody in the world from the President of the United States, to the bus boy at the local greasy spoon.

Why did it take me so long to get over being nervous and anxious? Frankly, a couple of decades of living helped. But behind it all was a new self confidence. I was a novelist. I'd sold novels to New York Publishers. I'd written syndicated columns in newspapers and trade magazines. I'd had stories about me in the local big town newspaper.

It would have been so much easier if I'd only had this self confidence and mind-set about 30 years earlier! The secret seems to be in knowing what you can do, knowing who you are, and knowing that you're just as good as anybody else out there in the whole universe. It all might not be exactly true, but it sure helps you get things done.

Anxious? Admit it. Take those two deep breaths. Then stand up and tell your boss that you're doing the work of someone two pay levels above you, that you're saving the company money, and you should have that $100 a week raise.......(good luck.)

Talking to the boss is one thing, but the toughest job most of us ever have is visiting with and comforting someone who is terribly ill or someone grieving over the death of a loved one.

If you're up to it, take a look at the next chapter and you'll find some workable, practical helps.

13

TALKING TO THE GRIEVING, THE ILL, THE DISABLED:

The hardest task most of us ever undertake is talking to a friend who has just lost a loved one. Death comes to all of us, but when it is unexpected or at an early age it is a double shock to those left behind.

Those grieving present a special problem for anyone who wants to talk to them, and comfort them. There are as many different ways to show grief as there are people. To show your respects and to help the grieving party, a personal visit is always best. The telephone just can't communicate the depths of feelings that are needed.

Some people will react to a death by being stoic, hold in their anger and fury and grief. For these people a logical approach is best. This entails the "business" of death. Can you help her with any arrangements? Can you call the newspaper with an obituary? Can you notify any friends or relatives? Can you bring in dinner for her for the next week? Are there any immediate bills that need to be paid or any small chores that need to be done at once or in the near future?

Talking to a grieving person is as much what you do as what you say. Just being there helps.

For the "business" of death for the stoic, you might ask about the will, any papers that need to be signed, any other business that needs to be taken care of? Has an executor for the estate been established? Some people want to do all of these things almost at once after a death. Others don't want even to think about them for months afterwards.

With most of these stoic types, they will break down sooner or later and cry. In this case crying is a cathartic to help cleanse the mind of the anger that is there. It will never answer the question of "Why did he have to die?" or "Why did he have to die so young?". But crying often helps a person to let go and start functioning again on her or his own.

Many of those who grieve want to be held and comforted. The enfolding arms of a friend can mean a lot at this time. It represents life, the continuation of society, the fact that someone is there to help them and bridge over the grief to find a renewed life without the loved one.

One good way to help a grieving person is to remind them of the wonderful life the deceased person had. They had many years of a good life, with a wonderful family, children, work that they enjoyed and successes. If the person had been in great pain toward the end, it's always good to mention that the loved one has been released from the terrible pain that had distorted the life and personality of the person toward the end. Now that's all over and he can be remembered as happy and joyful.

If a close friend has lost a spouse or other relative, it's good to offer friendship with that person before the funeral, but also be sure to continue to ask if you can help and make yourself available to them after the rites. Many people feel the shock of loss the most just after the burial.

That is often when they need the most support. They go home to an empty house. The relatives who came for the funeral have hurried back to their places and different parts of the country, and the jolt of living alone now in a house where you had a mate for thirty years is devastating.

This might be the time to help them put away the belongings and clothing of the lost one. An occasional dinner at your home or at a restaurant, a drive in the country, an outing to a play or concert are all things that you can do to help a friend overcome the loss of a loved one.

One last important suggestion. If you know the deceased, handle your own grief first, cry, yell, swear, pray, do whatever you need to do vent your own grief. Then you'll be able to watch your friend and see what he or she needs from you to help in handling this traumatic time in his or her life.

After death comes the grief, and then the agony of the loss in the survivor's daily life, and this is the time when a good friend can step in and be a spark and a savior. This is the time to build for the future, to highlight the fact that life must go on, there is much to do yet, to see, to live for. A good friend will help the bereaved to build the bridge over this chasm.

THE TERMINALLY ILL:

Almost as difficult as being a friend to a grieving person is to visit with the terminally ill. You both know the person is going to die. What can you say? What kind of a "face" should you present to this person?

I had a friend who was dying of prostate cancer. He had the operation, but it was too late and the cancer had spread into a dozen parts of his body. He had wasted away to a shadow of himself and it was hard to look at him.

I tried not to let on. Charlie was a fisherman, and we had taken numerous fishing trips on half day boats off the coast into the Pacific ocean and longer trips down along the Baja California, Mexico coast.

The fishing had been good lately just off the coast and

he mentioned hearing about it on the radio. We started telling fishing stories.

"Remember that winter day we were bottom fishing off La Jolla and you got seasick, but you had a good bite," I asked. He grinned, his eyes shone.

"Damned near heaved my guts out over the rail," he said.

"Yeah, and at the same time you were pulling in the winning jackpot fish, a seven pound ling cod. That was the second time in a row you beat me out of the jackpot."

We laughed until we cried. The afternoon rushed past as we talked about twenty years of good fishing trips. We didn't miss the time the coast guard helicopter had to rush out fifty miles to sea to pick him up in an aluminum basket on a long cable as the chopper hovered overhead. It was a severe attack of one of his ailments and it nearly killed him there on the boat.

"Remember how we got you on the basket and strapped in, and they hoisted you about fifty feet up in the air toward the chopper. You turned and waved at the rest of us on deck."

Charlie grinned and he laughed more than I had heard him laugh in a month.

We talked fishing for the rest of the afternoon. When I left, his wife trailed me outside and hugged me. She thanked me for coming and for giving Charlie the best afternoon he'd had in six months. She made me promise to come back the next day so we could talk about the time they tried to teach my wife and me to play bridge. That had produced as much laughter as the fishing trip stories.

Sometimes it doesn't take much to lift the spirits of a sick person. Most have little to look forward to, but they have a host of wonderful memories. All you have to do is figure out how to get them to remember the good times, the happy days, and that will make the present a little less difficult.

One day I came to visit him and I found Charlie's door closed and inside his room was empty. The nurse on duty told me that my friend had died during the night. I was saddened, but I was glad that I had helped make his last few days a little more pleasant.

DEALING WITH THE DISABLED:

I saw a sign on a bus for the handicapped. On the side was the word "disabled," but it was printed "dis ABLED." That sums up how most of people who are bound to a wheel chair or who walk with a crutch or a brace or who can't walk at all feel.

Most are adamant about being ABLED to do many things. A friend of mine suffered a bicycle accident when he was 18 years old and was paralyzed from the waist down. He had dreamed of becoming an optometrist.

He did. He went through college, and then optometry school and opened his own practice. He became virtually independent. He married, raised adopted children, drove a specially equipped car and commuted to his downtown office each day. He scooted from the car into his wheelchair and rolled himself into his office.

All day he worked helping people to see better. He was well into his sixties before his health forced him to sell his practice. Here was a man who was abled.

I have another friend who lived in Michigan and worked as a fireman. He had a fall and injured his back. Two years later he was declared physically unfit to continue as a fireman. He was given a medical retirement.

At the time he was 44, a relatively young man. He tried several jobs but couldn't seem to find something that didn't hurt his back. Now he stays home all day, takes care of the house, does the shopping, waters the lawn, does the laundry. He also goes for a three mile jog three times a week. Somehow he doesn't think he can find a job for which he is abled.

Most of the people I know who are disabled want you to treat them the same way you treat anyone else. Look them in the eye, say hello and smile. Chances are they'll smile back. If they have a disfigured face or palsy or are retarded, that's all the more reason to smile and say hello. It's almost for certain that they'll be smiling in their hearts even if you can't see it.

Remember, the most brilliant man in the world? It was a few years back. He had some debilitating disease that had worn away at him until he sat in a wheelchair and could communicate only through an electronic device. He was considered so brilliant that he confounded the greatest minds of our time. Yet for several years he could barely speak and communicated with a keyboard. He overcame his handicap and functioned right up to his untimely death.

The next time you see handicapped people, treat them the same way you would anyone else, and be sure to look them in the eye, smile and say hello.

If you've ever known anyone who was deaf, you know that you need to take special care when speaking with them. My grandmother was totally deaf. She learned to read lips when she was a young woman. When she was in her seventies she stayed with us sometimes. She was an excellent lip reader, that's how she raised seven of ten children after she went deaf overnight.

Sometimes at dinner I would catch her glance and say something, only I would simply mouth the words without saying the sounds. She looked around the table to see if anyone else was reacting to what I said and then she would laugh and shush me, saying "You're doing that again."

Most partially deaf people learn to read lips to help faulty and poor hearing. Remember you must be facing them so they can see you talk. Slow down, talk distinctly so your lips will form the words correctly.

With people who are hard of hearing, you may need to slow down as well as speak a little louder. Many of us get in the habit of mumbling and speaking softly when we should be doing just the opposite.

Sign language used by the deaf mute is a special skill which I wish I knew. It's a special way to communicate with some tremendously special people.

A common speech defect that many people have is stuttering. This is a disorder that impairs to various degrees a person's ability to communicate verbally. There are many reasons why people stutter, and a host of theories what stuttering actually is and how it can be helped.

A psychiatrist friend of mine told me that the unbreakable rule when talking to a person who stutters is *never finish a sentence or supply a missing word for them.*

Another good rule is never give such a person advice how to overcome the problem. They have heard all the old wives tales remedies and the quackery solutions, and even the medical therapies.

Never tell a stutter to slow down, to take it easy, to breathe deeply or to relax. This will only make the person more aware of the problem and could multiply it. One more suggestion. Don't change the subject or go for a drink or even move. Maintain eye contact with the person in silent support.

Who is in that much of a rush, anyway? I always tell people when I'm waiting in line that it's no big deal — I have another forty years to live, what's five more minutes here in line?

There are more hard conversations you'll need to carry on with your friends. Not a lot of fun, but sometimes these situations need to be faced. How do you talk to friends about unpleasant things such as drugs, alcohol and Aids? That's right, turn to the next chapter.

14

DIFFICULT AREAS TO TALK ABOUT

There are a lot of "sensitive" areas that often we must talk about in conversations. These are not counting politics and religion. When you talk about either one of those, somebody ends up getting angry, preaching or politicking and none of those results are what we want in polite conversations.

Other sensitive and difficult areas of human experience are ones that we can and should talk about. These include drugs, alcohol, AIDS, dieting, keeping secrets, people who lie, and racial and sexual slurs. Let's look at these one at a time:

THE NEW DEVIL — DRUGS:

Illegal drugs are the current deadly scourge riding America and a lot of the rest of the world. How to control, reduce and stop the use of drugs has become a vital and desperate need in most communities.

Government, laws and enforcement are another subject. You should do all you can to help them. Where you sometimes are confronted with drugs on a personal level it becomes a much harder thing.

How can you talk to someone about drugs? If you have

a child or a friend who is on drugs, it's your responsibility to that person to speak up. Someone said the greatest evil is when good people do nothing about bad things.

If you have a child on drugs you must confront him or her. You must learn all you can about drugs. You must seek help and counseling. Your responsibilities here are plain, and painful but at least you have a clear path to follow. But how do you talk to a friend about drug use?

The best way is to be blunt and up front.

"George, the most stupid thing you've ever done is to start doing drugs. If you keep on doing drugs, I simply won't see you again. We're through. If you want to continue our relationship, quit drugs. Period."

Drastic? You bet. That's all that works with some people. Later you might soften your stand and say that you'll help him go to counseling and to a detox program and offer support. The hard facts are most druggers don't want to quit. They might say they'll try it, but if they're hooked it will take more than a friend or a lover to persuade them.

What do you say to those who ask you to use drugs? A polite no is your first step. If they insist you have a right to insist back. Try this.

"Hey, you ragging me to try a joint. I've got the same right to tell you not to do a joint. How you gonna like that? Everytime you ask me to snort or to drink, I'm going to yell at you that you shouldn't be doing that. How are you gonna like that, fried brain?"

Extreme? Sure, but logical. If somebody asks you to do something you don't want to do, you have the same right to ask them to quit drugs, something they don't want to do. This type of confrontational defense isn't for the weak or shy. It takes guts to stand up for what you believe.

It can work. After the second time you're asked to shoot a line you tell them in a loud voice that they're stupid to be shooting coke and that they should stop. This can really put a crimp in the drug use at a party. Nobody wants to be the subject of your diatribe against them, so nobody else will ask you to use a needle.

If the people say that everyone else is shooting up, so why are you acting so standoffish, you'll probably want to get your coat and leave the party. Now it becomes a task of finding new friends who aren't hopheads and don't insist that you join them in their gradual slide into drug-induced poverty, loss of family and friends and job and eventually the biggest loss of all, of their misspent lives.

If you're uncomfortable in a group that is always drinking or doing drugs, it would be much better for you to get away from that group and make new friends who think more the way you do.

Peer pressure is powerful only as long as you stay in that peer group. It's easy to leave one group when you feel this way. It means that the people you thought were your good friends, really weren't, or they would respect your opinions and tell their other friends to respect your stands as well. You'll be better off to drop that bunch of losers and move to a group where you feel more comfortable.

THE OLD SEDUCER, ALCOHOL:

More misery, crime, broken homes, ruined marriages, broken relationships and tragedies come from the old seducer, alcohol, than from the current drug craze. That's probably because it's been around longer and has had more time to do more damage.

If you're in a situation where everyone is drinking but you, and you get pressured, use the same tactics as against the drug folks.

More and more people these days are accepting the "I don't drink," explanation. Records show that consumption

139

of beer and alcohol per capita is down. But still you will find situations where you wish you had stayed home. If you don't drink, tell them. One way around this is to ask for a soft drink, any of the colas, and no one will know what you're drinking.

If push comes to embarrassment, simply saddle up your horse and ride for home. Then look for a new set of friends who will let you, be you.

AIDS, THE PANIC DISEASE:

The mere mention of the word AIDS can bring a whole room to silence. The tremendous emotional/panic syndrome that surrounds this disease and the connotations and the still certain death from it once it attacks the immune system fully, is an awesome modern phenomenon.

The AIDS subject is the most sensitive of anything that can be discussed these days. Even in our "enlightened" sexual discussions, AIDS is still the monster in the closet.

AIDS is so controversial because it goes to the core of basic human behavior, sexuality. For several years AIDS was mainly transmitted through male homosexuality. Then the drug culture became infected and now the sharing of unsterilized needles for drug injection is responsible for a large number of AIDS cases.

Now women as well as men are infected and we're getting transmittal into the bi-sexual and the heterosexual communities.

The AIDS infections from the use of tainted blood transfusions has about stopped, but still there is a low grade terror even at this level.

How do you talk about AIDS? It depends who you're talking to. Certainly parents should make their children aware of the disease. Teenagers should be well acquainted

with what AIDS is, that it is transmitted by sexual contact
and through the use of shared drug needles. It should be
pounded into their heads that these are the methods that
produce 99% of all of the cases of AIDS.

AIDS and sexual activity must be tied together, and this
brings up another touchy subject, especially for parents of
teenagers.

The real tragedy is when a teenager gets AIDS and he
looks at his parents and says: "Why didn't you tell me about
this deadly disease?"

Tell them.

TO DIET OR NOT TO DIET:

A lot of people are on and off diets these days. It's a national
craze. The sad fact is that most diets don't work and don't
last. People's weight goes up and down like a balloon in
a thunderstorm.

Weight with most people is the touchiest subject of all.
Criticize my hair or my clothes, but don't mention a single
word about my being a tiny bit overweight. (150 pounds
or so)

If the chunky person brings up her weight, what do you
say? If you agree with her, she'll be mad. If you ignore
the problem you'll look insensitive. Try to tightrope walk
the center line. If you're on a diet yourself, this is a good
way to get yourself into the problem side of the picture
and you can commiserate together.

"Honey, do I look too fat to you?"

This is a question that should be dealt with only by a
lover or a psychiatrist. You're dead almost any way that
you answer it.

Some people make jokes about their own weight. The
psychologists tell us this is one way a fat person can take

the pressure off you, and at the same time complain a little publicly about their problem. Most are crying out for some kind of help.

The only kind of weight reduction program that works, is one that permanently changes the eating habits of the individual. The change is usually in the amount and the type of food the person eats and how many times a day, they eat. These programs are not "diets" in the normal sense. They are weight loss plans that do seem to get the weight off and if the principles used up to that point are followed, they will keep the weight off.

This weight talk reminds me of a friend of mine who said one night his wife was feeling mellow, and she told her husband if there was anything about her he didn't like, he should tell her and she'd change it to how he liked it.

He put her off half a dozen times, and each time she assured him she wouldn't get mad. Finally after many sweet inducements, the man said there was one thing she might work on.

She assured him she wouldn't be angry if he told her.

"You're just a little bit too heavy," he said.

His wife locked him out of the house for three days.

SECRETS YES; SECRETS NO:

How in the world do you handle the age old problem of secrets? This isn't only a highly sensitive situation, it can be explosive.

A friend should be a real friend before you tell them a secret you don't want spread all over. On the other hand if you don't want to hear secrets, you are perfectly within the good bounds of friendship to hold up your hands and say:

"Please, no secrets. I'm not able to keep them and you'll wind up getting furious with me, so please, please, don't tell me your secrets."

This is a good way to preserve a friendship.

If you have some deep dark secret you just must get off your chest, the best way is to tell a psychologist, a clergyman, your lawyer or a psychiatrist. Here your secret is safe. Not even the courts or a judge or the police can make one of these professionals reveal your secret even if it is about a double ax murder three days ago. This is what is known as privileged information, or client-clergyman and lawyer-client information which can't be revealed. The same is true for the psychologist and psychiatrist's talks with their patients.

More trust is put into secret telling than anything else. Be sure your friend is a good one and that you plan on keeping that friend for a long time before you reveal any secrets that could have a long life. If you and that friend have a parting of the ways, your secret will undoubtedly be spread around.

Teenagers probably have more trouble with "secrets" than anyone else. Most of these are devastating at the time, but on reflection a few years later seem trivial. Don't try to tell a teenager that now of course.

The best thing to do about secrets? Don't make it any secret that you simply don't have any secrets.

HOW TO HANDLE A LIAR:

I had a neighbor once who was also a good friend. We played pool at his table or mine, we went to football games, we neighbored across the street and back. One day he went to Los Angeles with a friend on a two day fishing trip.

I had been doing some ocean fishing and I wished that he would ask me to go along, but he didn't. When he came back he proudly displayed a fish fillet that weighed eight pounds and was fully two feet long. I knew it had to come from a big fish.

He told me it was half of the fillet from a ten pound yellow tail tuna he had caught about twenty miles off shore. I knew that he was lying. That big a fillet couldn't come off a yellow tail that small. Besides, the flesh of the fish itself was the wrong color and the wrong texture. I'd caught enough yellows to know that.

He said he'd split the yellow with his friend so they both could eat fish for weeks. Should I have challenged him in front of his wife and kids? I didn't. I watched and waited.

His marriage was breaking up, but I didn't know it. A month later he came over and asked my advice. He said he met this knockout of a woman in Los Angeles when he was on a trip for his company. He'd bought her a five hundred dollar ring and she kept asking for more.

He then admitted that the fishing trip was just an excuse to be away from home for two nights so he could spend them with the woman in L.A. He admitted that he had bought the fish fillet in a fish market at the harbor.

Then I knew why he was lying. Should I have spoken up a month earlier? Either way the damage was done. It turned out my neighbor was a slick pathological liar. He could make you believe anything he said. He was polished and smooth and an excellent salesman. He simply lied too much.

He was different from anyone I've ever met. Most people tell those "little white lies" to cover up for someone or they exaggerate a little, or they lie to protect someone. Usually this kind of untruth does little damage. It can even be beneficial such as lying to someone on her deathbed about one of her children who had car trouble and wouldn't make it home. In reality the bum was on a two day drunk and nobody could find him.

Lying can be a practiced art by a few, but for most of us lying makes us extremely uncomfortable. We might shift our glance frequently, we might start to perspire, we might move around on our chair. Our mind isn't at all happy with what our dumb mouth just said and our body is getting back at us.

If you run into someone who is downright lying, and you know it, you have two choices. You can confront them and give the correct information, or you can simply turn and walk away without any explanation. Either way it's a hard situation trying to figure out what to do especially if the lie is harming someone.

RACIST, ETHNIC, SEXUAL SLURS:

We've come a long way in developing tolerance. When I think of the difference in attitude between my father's views on race and ethnic matters and my son's, it's an amazing quantum jump. Still we have those individuals who snarl out invectives against races and certain ethnics and some who still take cheap shots against women.

What are you supposed to do when it happens in the conversation going around in your close group of six? Most of us abhor all kinds of slurs, put downs, and jokes aimed in any of these three directions.

You can be a crusader and a confrontationalist. I heard about a rabid feminist who suffered through three or four sexist jokes making women the butt of the laughter. At last she walked up to the man who was telling the jokes and smashed her fist hard into his crotch. Her aim was precise.

The man doubled over, screeched in agony and fell to the floor, pulling his legs up into a ball to try to temper the terrible pain of a ruptured testicle.

The woman stared down at the man. When he looked at her she snorted. "I bet you won't have the balls to talk that way again about woman," she said and stalked off.

Most men aren't that insensitive to women these days.

Neither are most women that motivated, but there is a middle ground.

When slurs of any of these three types are made, it's important for someone in the group to speak up.

"Come on, John. That was in terrible taste. You didn't really mean to say that."

A comment like this will often bring a retraction by the offender and in a few minutes, he'll slink away from the group where he's been embarrassed.

When the Polish jokes were so widespread, I had a Polish friend who took each one to heart. At last whenever he heard the start of a Polish joke he would hold up his hand.

"Hey, I'm Polish, and if this joke is insulting to Poles, I'm going to take off my coat and beat your brain out." Since Janos was a little over six-four and looked like a linebacker for the Chicago Bears, we had absolutely no Polish jokes told when he was around.

Such drastic action isn't required, but it's effective. A frown will often do wonders. Often such talk can be stopped by a comment such as: "What a crude thing to say," or "This conversation has dropped to a new low," or "What ever happened to *polite* conversation."

If the bigot persists in the slurs and slanders, turn and walk away. When enough people do this, the sexist, racist outlaw pig will be left talking to himself and the wall.

Touchy subjects can come in a variety of guises. The one thing they all have in common is that they involve people. Most people are much more fragile and easily hurt that we think. We don't always see the hurt. Try to talk and shape your words in a manner so they won't embarrass, hurt or depress anyone. Then you'll have the perfect method for handling any sensitive subject that you experience.

Someone asked me one day if there are special ways to phrase things when speaking to men and women. Guess what I told him? Turn the page to the next chapter and find out.

15

WHAT ABOUT MAN-WOMAN TALK?

First let me say, I'm all for it, man-woman talk. Most relationships start out with conversation. You meet someone who is attractive and pleasant and you say Hi and start to talk. You go through all of the methods of good conversation and three months later, you're still seeing this person.

How did this all happen? Mostly through talk, at least it started out that way.

You better keep talking if you want that good relationship to continue.

How many husbands and wives have you heard say: "But we never TALK with each other any more?"

You must hear that a lot. As relationships grow and mature and even mellow, talking takes on a less and less important part. Things are simply understood, or known and taken as a matter of course. The relationship becomes what many psychologists call, "comfortable", you know him and he knows you and you talk to plan and work out programs and projects, but you don't need that minute to minute running dialogue that you did when you first met.

Then you were getting to know each other, probing, asking, answering, questioning, wondering, dreaming. That aspect is definitely over. So what comes between the questioning and wondering and the "comfortable" phase?

147

SOME BASIC TRAINING:

From the earliest times in our lives, little boys and little girls are interested in and talk about different things. Boys talk more about their activities, about games, about the woods or the street, about the creek or the playground. As they get older they talk about who is the best at the games, who can run the fastest, climb the tree, swing the highest, who can jump out of the swing and land the farthest out.

This boy talk about things and activities tends to extend well into the teen years and even beyond where a lot of it is still about games -- professional and college sports, fishing and hunting, racing.

Little girls, on the other hand, are more likely to play with one or two companions instead of in a group as boys do. They often concentrate their talk on their dolls, and they treat them as people. This leads to the older girls talking about their friends, the girls in their classes, the boys in the school.

They are more people oriented than boys are, and this behavior, too, continues into grade and high school and beyond. These different interests can come into sharp contrast and conflicts when junior high boys and girls begin to become aware of each other.

"Mom, I didn't know what to talk about with Jimmy," Wanda wailed to her mother.

She didn't. Of course, neither did Jimmy know what to talk about with Wanda, so it was a rather silent walk home from school. During junior high and high school, boys and girls slowly learn a few things from each other and get a glimmer how to talk to these strange creatures of the opposite sex.

It usually takes a long time for a boy to realize that a girl, that soft, flighty, silly, persons-you-can't-hit, wonderful little things, are really *people*, and a lot like themselves. Girls don't have quite this same hangup and wonder why boys are so shy and standoffish.

All of this, too often, carries over into the adult world. Some men will meet a pretty girl at a party and right away start talking about the baseball season, or his upcoming hunting trip, or the new engine he just put in his sports car. Really things the woman wants to talk about, right?

On the other hand the girl might be dying to talk to someone about the new see-through blouse a girl from public relations wore. How could she do that? It was *so revealing.* She even saw Harold there with a girl from personnel! She didn't even know that Harold ever went to personnel. How did he catch that particular blonde's eye? She wondered if the girl turned him down the first time. She looked like the type, all fluffy hair and thigh high skirts and gold chains enough to choke a giraffe, and....

The sexes seem traditionally to go in opposite directions when it comes to conversations. That is until they realize how important this matter of talking and communicating really is if one of them wants to have a satisfying and long lasting relationship with the other one.

ADVANCED MAN/WOMAN TALK:

Now, you have some idea of the problems of carrying on a reasonably dignified conversation with this fantastic girl you have just met. You even ask a few ritual questions, and one of the first things you find out is that she loves to ride horses. You've done some extra work in movies as a rider and done some stunt riding so you're off and running talking about horses and riding.

What you realize you must do is to ask some more probing questions and then concentrate on what she is interested in. If she's smart, the girl will be doing the same thing right back at you. She might hate the whole idea of fishing, but if you're hooked on it, she's going to try to find something about it to talk about.

Is this pushing? Is this being phoney? Is it dishonest? Not really. You're expanding your horizons, you're on a mission to learn all you can about the other person. Quickly you may find out that this large male beast with the hunk body and handsome face is a nut about gardening and chess and ballet. The more things you can find out about him, the more you can break down the male/female stereotypes, and get on to doing some honest talk about things perhaps you both enjoy.

DO YOU HAVE AN ATTRACTIVE VOICE?

Let's talk about something you never think about: your voice. Many times a person will be annoyed and end a conversation quickly because he or she simply can't stand the voice of the other person. So he's a hunk or she's a knockout, the voice is so irritating that's the only thing you can think about.

In these cases, it's not really what you're saying that hurts you, it's the way that you say it.

Do a little self evaluation here. Do you have any of these problems with your voice and speaking:
- Mumble or talk too softly.
- Use poor grammar or mispronounce words.
- Talk in a high pitched, irritating voice.
- Interrupt others when they talk.
- Have a thick foreign or regional accent.
- Talk with a heavy nasal whine.
- Talk much too loudly.
- Pepper your talk with swear or curse words.

• Use a low, monotonous voice.
• Overuse crutch phrases: You know, like, well.

This is a good time for some self evaluation. All of these vocal traits and conversation boo boo's will hurt you in a conversation with anyone. If you have a tendency to interrupt others, make a concentrated effort not to. If you know you talk too much and too loudly, listen to yourself as you talk. Try talking to your mirror and listen as you speak. This is a great way to work on your voice, as well as your smile and your nod and other conversational visual helps.

A little work here on one of your problems can make a big difference when you talk to that next sweet young thing at that party coming up.

GRADUATE COURSE 204: NICE:

So, how can you further entice this knockout in the mini skirt and see through blouse? Your first job after the introductions and the start of the ritual questions is to put this sweet thing at ease, make her feel comfortable talking with you.

How to do this? Turn on your natural charm. First use good eye contact. Let her know that you're interested in talking more. Be expressive in your voice, not dullsville, but upbeat and interested in her. Ask just enough questions so she knows that you're interested but not so many she thinks you're with the FBI or the local vice squad.

Use a warm tone in your voice. Let her know that you're interested in what she's saying and that you wouldn't mind sitting there the rest of the night talking to her. Keep in mind what she's saying and let her know she has your complete attention.

Now, that wasn't so hard. Yes, that's charm. Most of

charm is being thoughtful of the other person and doing things that they like and enjoy and make them think they are the best conversationalist in the world.

HOW HONEST CAN YOU BE?:

Okay, let's say you met him, the talk has gone well, you've let him know you're interested in him, and you have good eye contact and he's brought you a drink and you've been talking about a lot of things, several of which you have a mutual liking for. What's next? Just how honest can you be with this guy?

You know you'd like to see him again. You want to get to know him better. Can you tell him so?

Most psychologists say that at this point, honesty indeed is the best policy. You might say:

"Ron, I'm enjoying our talk, I'm really attracted to you." If that's too forward for your style, you might try:

"Ron, I've enjoyed our talk. We have a lot of things in common. I can relate to a lot of the things you've said."

There, you said it. That wasn't so hard. If he's anything like the *wunderkind* you think he is, he'll pick up on your slightly obtuse indicator and say something of the same thing.

At this point don't play the dating game. Don't try to be something that you're not just for that first date. If you are phoney at this point, neither one of you will enjoy your first and last date together.

Instead keep it honest all the way. If you are available and interested, make it easy for him to ask you out for coffee or lunch. If he doesn't do the inviting, strike out on your own like this:

"Ron, I've had a great time talking to you tonight. We work close together down town. Why don't we get together for lunch next week, say Wednesday?"

You've never asked a man to lunch or anywhere? Come on, lady, this is the 1990's. You don't have to sit like a small pretty flower in the edge of the garden and wait for some big strong man to come along and pick you. Use your wings and fly a little, that's why you have wings.

NO SALE:

What if your best efforts seem to be slamming against a stone wall? The girl is attractive, small and pert, cute and dances like a dream. But she seems unresponsive to your hints you'd like to see her again.

Your signals seem to be all wasted. She's polite and thanks you graciously when you compliment her, but she doesn't make eye contact with you much, and she seems to be looking around a little. Maybe this isn't a good time to ask her to lunch the next day. She works in your building and it would be easy, but she just isn't showing any enthusiasm for you.

So, thank her for the talk, indicate you need to see the hostess about something, and move on. Hey, you can't make every sale. Ring up a mental "no sale" and move on. There are a dozen pretty girls at this party and at least half of them are single. Charge into the fray and take your best conversational shots. Who knows, maybe the next time.

IT USED TO BE EASIER:

In the early 1900's it was much easier to tell if a young man was interested in a young girl. She might drop her handkerchief near him, but more likely she would give him shy glances from a safe position with three or four other girls. If there was some attraction and the young man was interested, he would return her handkerchief and later call on her father and ask if he could come courting.

Fathers reacted differently then just as they do now. If he thought his daughter was too young, the boy got the heave ho and that ended it. If the girl was old enough, the father might ask her if she was interested in seeing the boy.

Back then there were plain to follow, hard and fast rules about meeting, courting, getting to know each other.

Now the only rule is that there are no rules. The glance across a crowded room still seems to be a time honored route to meeting new people. On the other hand walking up and pushing out a delicate hand, a great smile and a, "Hi, I'm Julie and I've been wanting to meet you," is a much easier way.

Remember there are no rules. Remember when you're being the more forward one, you have to be ready for some rejections and brush offs, whether you're a man or a woman when you make the first move. But that's no problem.

I knew a salesman once who had as his slogan: "You make enough calls you'll make enough sales." A cold canvas salesman can expect only one sale in twenty calls. A Hollywood actor trying for a commercial might get cast in one out of 50 auditions. That's 49 rejections for one success. Now *that* is rejection.

By now your odds sound pretty good. March up and smile and say Hi and introduce yourself and give it a try. In nine out of ten times, you're going to have a satisfying conversation with a new person. That's not saying it will result in a lunch and then a dinner and then a relationship and then marriage and six kids, and twelve grandchildren and retirement in the country, but it's a start.

CONTINUING EDUCATION:

Just as people are never through learning, we should also keep learning about how to keep our man/woman relationships alive and well and productive. No one has all of the answers, because people come in millions of different styles, moods, forms, and with various desires, needs and problems.

However, here are some ways that others have found work to help keep a man/woman relationship alive and growing through the weeks, months and years.

• *Learn to be a good listener.* This is probably the most important point. Just as you started showing interest in the other person, continue to show that interest by really listening to what he is saying.

Don't try to listen when you're doing something else. Stop and turn and make eye contact and touch the other person and make sure that you give your total undivided attention to what they are saying. Listen and remember.

It might not seem important to you, but to the other person it may be tremendously important otherwise they wouldn't have bothered you with it.

When you listen, apply it at once. What can you do about this situation or problem? How can you help your partner? What is the real reason for this talk? Is it something more than the immediate problem?

Listen and react and try to remedy any problems if you can. If it isn't a problem situation, just a talk about the day, it's still important to the other person or it wouldn't have been brought up. So listen commiserate, and communicate your understanding.

Try not to prejudge what the other person is going to say. Listening is the key. Listen not only to what is said, but how it is said as well. Many times that is as important, or more important than what is being said.

• *Talk it over, talk it out.* I mentioned before about talking with your important other. Most relationships start off with conversations and ritual questions. Then when we think we know enough about the person, the questions taper off.

A few weeks of questions aren't enough. I write novels and I have a character definition chart that I use to get to know my characters. There are 54 questions that I ask and then answer about each of my top four or five characters. By the time I'm through with those questions, I know that character much better than I know any of my friends. My wife says I know them better than I do her.

We never know enough about our mates. Even though we move out of the interrogation and get acquainted phase, couples must keep on talking to each other. Yes, we communicate in other ways, but talking is still the one way that mankind has an advantage over the other animals.

Life must be shared on a daily basis, even if you've been married twenty years and are in the "comfortable" stage of your relationship.

Sharing what happens regularly, keeps a couple closer together. We're friends with a couple in our neighborhood. I thought I knew Harry like an old shoe. Then one day he said if he had it to do over again he would have quit engineering school in his second year and gone to Boston where there was a cooking school he wanted to attend.

"I always wanted to be a chef," he said one day when we were fishing. "You never knew that about me, did you?"

I didn't. People are so complex and multilayered that most of us never truly understand ourselves, let alone a wife of forty years or a son or a daughter reaching middle age.

The secret is to keep talking. Some people talk over the day in bed just before they go to sleep. Some turn off the TV at meal time and have a rousing conversation with the kids. Some couples never talk at all and build higher and higher walls around themselves until the relationship has little reason for being.

Keep talking!

• *Share that big dream.* Secrets are fine, but not between a man and a woman, husband and wife. This close intimate relationship should include all of your dreams. No matter how impractical, how silly, how ridiculous your dreams are, you should be able to share them with your partner.

As a relationship deepens and lengthens, the more people are willing to open up with each other. This shows a maturity by the couple and could develop into a permanent relationship.

Usually the couple who can be the most open with each other, is also the happiest couple. They have no secrets, nothing to fear, nothing to hide. It creates a relaxed, honest attitude in which friendship and love can flourish.

The one rule on intimate secrets between a couple: Never, never use those secrets to scold, tease or chastise the other person. Using a secret against your partner to help win an argument could instead mean the end to a relationship. Secrets are meant to be shared in confidence, and never used in jest or in anger against the other person.

• *Don't demand, criticize, nag or blame.* Drill sergeants should stay in the Marines, not in the household. The best way to get everyone mad at everyone else is to start demanding things be done for you.

You get home. You're beat. You drop in your favorite chair, kick off your shoes. "Honey, bring me a cold Coke and the paper," you say in your cold office voice. Not even the "honey" on the front of an order softens it enough.

When I was in high school, the kids used to have a great saying. If somebody told them to do something, the comeback was always: "Oh, yeah? Who was your slave last year at this time?"

Instead of an order, make it a request in your best and most pleasing voice. "Hey, Pretty Lady. If you're still in the kitchen would you please bring me a cold Coke and some of those pretzels?" If this particular Pretty Lady is home from her nine to five job, she just might do it.

Another good way to smash up a relationship is to criticize, nag and blame the other person. Yes, there are a lot of two income families these days. Both of you get tired and cranky when you get home after a tough day, but don't take the frustrations of the office or the job out on each other.

If you feel you must criticize your mate about something, do it in a positive way and softly with an easy out for the other person.

"Bill, I wonder if we've been spending a little too much on sports and recreation lately. I know you like to ski and I go to the gym, but maybe we should look at the whole thing and get it back in proportion."

(Here Bill had been going skiing twice a week into the mountains and since Martha's twisted knee, she doesn't ski for a while. She included herself in the criticism and Bill decided that he wouldn't go up the mountain for a month or so, and they smoothed it over nicely.)

There are going to be disagreements, but never, never nag about something that bugs you. It's a fine way to end a happy relationship.

If you find yourself wanting to blame your exclusive other for something that went wrong, hold up a minute. Remember all of the great things he or she has done in the past, all of the fine qualities that the other person has. Remember all of the good points you know about your mate that made you fall in love in the first place. Take another look at the "blame" thing and pound it down into a trivial matter you can forget or ignore.

• *Always touch and sparkle.* A lot of women say their men never say, "I love you." It's always nice to hear, but how much better when it comes with some honest feeling.

A dull monotone can kill the words so it would be better not to say them.

You can use a simple e technique to sparkle up your conversations. Try putting a little upward inflection on the end of your greeting. It will get your mate's attention and usually bring a return greeting in the same happy vein.

The monotone greeting just shouts that the other person isn't happy to see you no matter what the words. Monotones have resulted in more ruined relationships than the mini skirt. Give your next hello to your absolute other the upward lilt at the end and just watch that person respond.

Touching, hugging, kissing are actions that seem to taper off in all long running relationships. It doesn't have to be that way. The "taking for granted" label jumps up at once. "You don't love me any more," she says. "You never kiss me any more."

The man side of these relationships has to remember that women honestly like all that hugging and kissing, and it's not only to be used just to get her into your bed for purposes other than sleeping.

A hug hello, a kiss goodbye, a little squeeze in between. What's it going to cost you? Give it a try and just watch the benefits start to roll in.

A few pages back I spoke about criticizing your spouse or live in. But what if you have a friend you really think you can help, but it's going to take some criticism? How can you do that and not get your fingers burned down to the knuckles? Turn the page to the next chapter and see.

16

PRACTICAL ASPECTS OF CRITICISM

Someone said that criticism breaks up more friendships than any other single element. They may be right.

No one likes to be criticized. When critical comments come, most of us want to strike back. "Hey, you're not so perfect either, you know." It's a natural reflex action. There are ways however that can be used to fend off criticism of yourself, and to offer criticism to a friend so the friend will accept it and benefit by it.

Psychologists and psychiatrists are what I call "professional critics." Their job is to tell us what's wrong with us and why. Most people accept criticism from a professional. They know they need some help or they wouldn't be on the couch in the first place.

But even a psychologist who gives criticism uses a special way of doing it. We'll talk about that later.

I work with a writers group. We're a bunch of selling novelists, plus a few who haven't sold yet. We call it a 'workshop' and what we do four hours a night, twice a month is offer criticism to our fellow members. This is literary criticism where there are no blacks and whites, where a lot of the comments by the people in the group can be sharp and tough, and where a thick skin is a requirement if you want to read some of your work.

Do we have lots of fights, hard feelings, jealousies and hair pulling scenes? No, and seldom any ruffled feelings. That's mostly because we've been doing this for 30 years and have learned how to take and give literary criticism properly.

Part of it is that we come there with the expressed idea of *being criticized.* Our members sign up in advance to be cut and slashed and riddled with criticism. Of our own free will we sit under a good light and read a chapter from a work in progress. It might be the first chapter of a new novel or a chapter that we're having trouble with.

We ask for it because we know members of this group are professionals and their comments are going to help make our novel better and make us more polished writers.

Since we go there with the *idea that we will be criticized,* we are ready for it. The criticism still hurts, you bet it does. When you read a chapter from "your baby" to the group you feel naked and that everyone is ganging up on you and throwing poison darts at you.

In this case we have an excellent group who criticize in a way that will help the story, that will help the writer, and we hope will lead to the sale of the novel.

Many of our best critics will start off this way: "Jim, I like your main character and your setting and background are right on target. The plot line works for me in getting this first chapter started. However....."

Most people open with some words of praise about the good parts of the chapter and the story. It helps lessen the blow of the critical comments.

Someone said that if you want to succeed at fiction writing, "You have to be able to kill your own babies." This refers to cutting out a character or a chapter, or an element that isn't right for the novel. It's hard. You created this character, this story, this bit of truth and wisdom.

Oh, we never let anyone read to the group the first time

that they come. We make sure that the writer knows the kind of professional criticism we give and they must understand we will be doing the same to their story. Those who can withstand honest criticism stay in the group, and most eventually publish their novels.

SOFTEN THE CRITICAL BLOW:

In the writer group, everyone knows we're criticizing the work for the good of the writer. With a friend this isn't a given and you have to pave the way, soften the blow, ease the thrust of the knife. You've heard the phrases before, but they are ideal and mandatory to use if you're criticizing a friend you want to remain a friend. Remember these:

• Phil, may I make a suggestion...."

• Jane, you know I'd never do something to hurt your feelings, but in this case I really need to say some things to you...."

• Walt, I have a suggestion to make that I think will be in your best interest...."

• Sally, I don't want you to be offended, but I've thought a lot about this and I think we're good enough friends that I can tell you."

• Joe, I'm on your side in this hassle with the old man, so please don't take what I'm saying as being against you."

With an opening like this, the person knows that something is coming that they might not really like. What you have to show them is that you support them, that you're their friend and that you really care about them.

None of us likes criticism, but if we can word it in endearing and positive ways, it will help take some of the sting out of the facts. Chances are that the person you're talking to knows of their problem, and will at least listen to what you have to say.

That's about all you can hope for. As with any criticism, it's always a good idea to have the hint of a solution to the problem, or some help for the one you're criticizing.

CONSTRUCTIVE CRITICISM:

What we're talking about here is "constructive criticism", the kind that can be used by the individual to correct bad habits, to do better on the job, to be more relaxed and at ease at social functions, to impress the boss so he'll be in line for the next raise or promotion.

Harping, nagging, jealous criticism is not what we're talking about. Anything that simply tears down a person or his habits or personality or work, is not helpful.

If someone says: "Lucy, you're terrible at parties," it doesn't really help Lucy much. She'll probably stop going to your parties.

If you say, "Lucy, I've noticed you standing alone at the party tonight with your legs crossed and your arms crossed and a frown on your face. Could I offer a suggestion? If you'll stand in a little more open posture, keep your arms at your side, and smile, you'll meet a lot more eligible men. Oh, and don't be afraid to make eye contact with that hunk you've been watching and smile and say, HI, when he comes over."

That is constructive criticism, with some good ways to take care of the problem. That's what constructive criticism is all about.

HOW CAN YOU BENEFIT FROM CRITICISM?

Let's say the critic is on the other foot. How can you benefit when someone criticizes you?

163

First, take a look at the one doing the critic work. Is this a friend who is truly being supportive, someone who cares for you and is concerned with your welfare? If so, you better hunker down and listen with your total attention. Maybe even take notes.

• listen carefully to the criticism.

• evaluate it without anger.

• check the ways your critic suggests that you take care of the problem.

• decide if you want to make the adjustment, change your behavior.

• figure out if the suggested solution will help you.

I knew a man who worked in a business. He was a middle ranking management man. His secretary was his confidant and she was worried about her boss. One day she closed the door to his office.

"How long have I worked for you, Mr. Johnson?"

"Three years."

"Right, and I want to work for you when you're vice president, but now I'm afraid you might not make it."

"Why? I have the best sales record in the place."

"True, but when I see you walk into those management meetings, I compare you with the others. Now, I know this might not be the right way to say it, Mr. Johnson, but I'm going to anyway. You need to give more attention to how you dress. Your suits are too old, dated. Your ties are out of style. You still wear white shirts when everyone else has colored shirts. I really want you to get that promotion, but I think a good review of your wardrobe would help."

Mr. Johnson thought about it. He nodded. "I know I'm not as sharp a dresser as some of the men. That's worried me. Now is the time to make a change. Thanks for the suggestion. What store do you think I should go to for my new look?"

He went to the store she suggested and bought a whole

new wardrobe. At least now he had a chance for the promotion and his secretary a chance to move up in her field to Executive Assistant.

What if the person criticizing you is not even a friend, is in competition with you for a job or position, and is well known around the office for generally bad mouthing everyone? Then you have to consider the source as part of your evaluation of the critical comments.

Don't automatically throw out what has been said to you. Sometimes our worst enemies can give us a clue about our lives, our behavior or our methods, that can be remarkably constructive. So evaluate every criticism, see if there is any truth or merit in it and then take any action that fits.

THE HYPER-CRITICAL DRUDGE:

Every once in a while we come across a person who simply delights in being hyper-critical. Nothing is right. Everything is sloppy or wrong, or too loud or too soft, or the wrong color, or not right politically.

Some of these people are professional complainers. They wouldn't feel right if they didn't have something or someone to run down, castigate or otherwise cut to shreds. When you run up against someone like this, there is little you can do but turn around and sail off in the other direction.

I had a friend once who took a combative stance against such a person. When he found one, he delighted in contradicting and taking exactly the opposite approach. If the detractor said the speaker went on too long and was dull, he would counter with how much he enjoyed the brilliant speaker and how he had read three of his books on the subject. Every single thing that our professional complainer attacked, my friend made a counterstrike on, extolling the virtues, beauty, usefulness and rightness of the project. It took only three such pointed and powerful counter attacks to jolt our complainer out of his seat and move him along to better complaining grounds.

MAKE CRITICISM WORK FOR YOU:

We all get criticized now and then. It's just part of living. The secret is not to strike out and defend yourself. Take a big gulp of air, blink a couple of times and then try to make the criticism of yourself you've just undergone work for you.

"You always have to be right in an argument. You never let the other guy win."

Tough stuff, right, when it's aimed at you. Take it and gulp once more. Most of the criticism we get is of a general nature. Like the one above. Try to get it defined a little more with a question.

"Well, I'd never thought of it that way. What do you mean that I always have to be right?" Here you're asking for some details of the particular point the other person is trying to make.

"Well, like just now. We were talking about ecology, and you said the ecology nuts were doing more to ruin the ozone layer than they are helping it. You didn't offer any proof, you just made the statement and refused to discuss it any more. I really don't think you believe that. You just wanted to win the argument."

Well, maybe the person has found something about the way I argue that can be helpful. Was I making a flat statement just to close out the talk about ecology and move on to something new? To him I sounded abrupt, egotistical and with a closed mind. Something to consider.

A good way to respond to criticism like this is to agree with the principle of the criticism. You might say.

"Well, I certainly didn't mean to sound so abrupt. I agree with you that a closed mind is a tremendous waste. Let me do some more thinking about the ecology matter and maybe we can talk about it some other time."

By agreeing with the thrust of the criticism you can blunt it, turn it around to say maybe they are right and that you'll certainly give their suggestion some more thought.

In most criticism, there is some germ of truth that you can agree with, at least in principle. If you get this far, it often takes the bite out of the other person's cutting criticism and they will tend to back off a little. This is especially valuable if you're in a family situation, or a group where you can't simply get up and leave. Then co-existence is a good plan and finding some truth in the criticism launched against you is a great way to defuse what could turn into hot and unkind words if left to grow into a larger controversy.

Another quick way to fend off criticism is to point out that everyone has a right to his or her opinion. In this way you're not saying that they are right or wrong, you're just saying that they can believe the way they want to, and you can still believe what you want to. Something like this:

"Boy, the politics in this town are rotten."

"Oh, I can see why you think the political situation here is so bad, but I think the best way to clean it up is for all of us to vote and to get involved with politics and work hard for the candidate we think will do the best job."

Here you have agreed with the person's right to his opinion, and then go on to share your position with him as well.

Again, this is a way to defuse a critical situation where you have strong opposing points of view and strong personalities.

THE ULTIMATE — SELF CRITICISM:

There used to be a party game that would have each person at the group write down the three best personality traits they had. Next they were told to write down the three character flaws that they had or behavioral problems that they wished they could correct.

The papers were not signed and then were collected by the hostess. At some groups the game was to read the person's best personality traits and the group as a whole would try to pick out the person. If no one could figure out who it was, the hostess then moved on to the three problems the person thought they had and the guessing went on again.

Usually no one could pick out the writers of the clues, and with good reason. Most of us hide our flaws and behavioral problems. On the other hand, the good traits we think we have may be hard for others to detect.

The game does bring up the idea of self criticism. Does it work and can anyone do it?

Every psychologist worth his or her Ph. D. sheepskin has a self evaluation test, or a self criticism test. I've always wondered if this is the kind of test that you can fail.

The doctor gives you a piece of paper, sometimes with lines and boxes on it and asks you to answer the questions. A composite of many of these tests might look something like this:

1. What aspects of your personal life do you think you should change?

2. What parts of your social life needs revamping?

3. What things about your business or professional life should be changed?

4. Are you happy with your physical appearance? What would you change if you could?

5. What are the things in your marriage and family life

that you would change?

Then in column two is space to write down the changes you want to or think you should make. In column three is space for you to show just how you can go about making those changes.

These tests are fun to fill out and play with. But after a few years of living and watching people, I'd bet a crock full of corn meal mush that most folks would never get around to making more than one or two of those changes they wrote down that they should make.

Reminds me of the story about the traveling salesman who was working in Nebraska farm country. He stopped his car alongside a dirt road and walked over to a field where a farmer was cutting hay. When the farmer came around with his tractor, he stopped, let it idle and walked over to the fence to see what the young man wanted.

"Sir, I've got here a set of Nebraska Agricultural Studies that show the best crops and the best methods for growing them that this state has ever seen. These books are the result of the state agricultural college's twenty year study. They're absolutely guaranteed to increase your farm production and your income by fifty percent."

The salesman beamed at the farmer who pushed the straw hat back on his head and wiped away the sweat. He snorted.

"Them books wouldn't do me a bit of good, young feller. Hell, I ain't farming half as good now as I know how."

Knowing and doing are two different things.

IS FREE ADVICE WORTH IT?

Criticism is a form of advice, you're pointing out a flaw or a problem and then if you're any kind of a friend at all, you carry through and make suggestions to overcome the flaw or solve the problem.

Someone said that free advice is usually worth about what it costs.

Many times when someone asks you to give them advice, what they really want is for you to support a position that they have already decided upon. In this case if your advice supports their position, they are pleased. If your advice is not what they hoped that you would say, it can lead to hard feelings and even the loss of a friend.

Giving advice at any time is risky, even when the person asks you for it. If you try to take it upon yourself to give advice when it isn't asked for, you run the risk of ruining a friendship or preventing one from starting.

If your friend Maria says: "Come on now, tell me what I should do about Larry." You are in a spot. You know she likes Larry and just because he's a rat and a two timer she doesn't think that's any reason not to go on seeing him.

How can you tell her? You might preface your advice with something to soften it and leave you the proverbial fire escape. Say something like:

"Now, Maria, you may not want to hear this..." or "I don't want you to get mad at me, but this is what I suggest that you do." Or "Remember, this is just my opinion..."

With this disclaimer in place start out slowly, try to get her approval as you go along.

"Now, Maria. I know you're head over heals in love with this guy and I don't expect to change your mind about him, but you asked me, so I have to be honest with you. You realize that Larry doesn't have a job don't you?"

"Yes, I guess so."

"You know that he's been seeing someone else. You told me you saw him out with some blonde two nights ago."

"Well, yeah, but that was his sister....I think."

"Maria, don't kid yourself. You know she wasn't his sister. I know it. Half the block knows it. It doesn't seem to me that a guy like Larry deserves a great woman like you. I might be wrong, Maria. But I think you should have a man who is a lot better and smarter, and who will treat you like a lady and be good to you.

"I'm sorry if I've hurt your feelings, but this is what I think. Maria, you deserve better than Larry."

By turning the thing around a little and making Maria the key to the discussion instead of Larry, it puts a new emphasis on what she deserves, rather than what a lout Larry is.

Even with logic and a soft approach like this, be ready for your friend to disagree with you and maybe scream at you and rush off mad. If she was looking for somebody to give her advice about what she had already decided to do, stay with Larry, then there's no way you can win.

So, give advice?

• Only when you get pinned down.

• Never volunteer advice, you risk losing a friend.

• Use a softening disclaimer phrase before your advice.

• Try and figure out if your friend is simply looking for someone who will agree with him or her.

• Be ready to run for cover, or lose a friend if you give advice your friend doesn't like.

How to handle criticism is important, and when it comes up in the office or where you work, it is harder yet. For a quick run down on some of the important aspects of making friends in business without getting fired, turn to the next chapter.

17

THE BUSINESS SIDE

Yes, there some special guidelines, protocol and common sense that apply especially to meeting people and making friends in the market place and in your business relationships.

Most people in business spend more waking hours at their place of work than they do at home. True. At work you're in a closed situation. You can't choose whom you work with, or your boss. You are presented with a job opportunity with almost all of the things that are important already spelled out and set in stone.

That means you accept your boss and see if you have a smooth understanding relationship with your fellow workers. Here more than ever you need to bring into play the open, friendly way of greeting people, the eye contact and the Hi, as you meet or pass in the hall.

Most of what has been covered in the chapters so far applies equally as well to business as to your social life. Be open and friendly, get to know the people you're working with and be careful about giving advice.

YOU AND YOUR BOSS:

The worry most people have is how to get along with their boss. If it's a structured situation, you'll probably have little contact with the big boss. The managers down the line will be the ones you deal with.

What to do here? The best suggestion is to "be yourself". Most management people can spot a phoney a mile and a half to Thursday. Be yourself and do your job. When the boss is around don't put on special surges of energy or do work you wouldn't do ordinarily just to impress him.

Do your job the best way you know how, be open and friendly with the boss. Make eye contact and say hello, and ask if there's anything you can do for him. One reason he is the boss and you're his worker, is that he has some talent, knowhow, experience or contacts which you don't have yet. Watch him and learn. No matter what level you're on, there's always lots of chances to learn from those working above you.

I had one boss who said her job was to teach her people to replace her. When she had someone who could do her job, then she would be ready to move up to do the job of her boss. A lot of business management people watch for people "on the way up." They like to see their workers taking responsibility, doing tougher jobs, taking some of the load off their shoulders.

Then your boss can say to his boss: "Hey, look how Jones is progressing. He's a good man and I've made him into an ideal management trainee to move up the ladder. I'm good with people. I help them to help me and it makes us all look good."

If you need to talk to the top man, it's a good idea to set up an appointment to see him. It depends what the situation is in your work place. If it's a foreman in a manufacturing plant, this might not be needed.

If you need to see the vice president in charge of marketing, ask his secretary when he can meet with you for fifteen minutes on a problem that needs his attention. You'll get the time and the meeting.

Be prompt, state your problem or give your information and hope for some reaction. When your time is up, or your message presented, stand up and get ready to leave. If you boss stands up when he's with you, usually it's his indication that the interview is over and it's time for you to get out of his office. Thank him for the time and get back to work.

Just because he's the boss is reason enough for some people to dislike him or her. The fact that the other person has authority over you is hard for some people to understand.

"I don't want nobody telling me what to do," is the attitude. For this person, a sheepherder's job in northern Montana might just be the perfect match with his personality.

Your boss is there for a reason. If you want his job, work at it and work with your boss, not against him.

Some supervisors like to have ideas, suggestions and even complaints from their people put in writing in the form of memos or notes. This way the boss has a record of it and it can be handled in the right fashion. Find out if your supervisor or boss wants a verbal contact or if he would rather see some paper first and then talk with you.

THE DREADED JOB INTERVIEW:

Some people would rather go to the dentist than sit down for a job interview. Exactly the opposite should be true. Here is an *opportunity* for you to show your stuff. Here is your chance to impress the one interviewing you with your knowledge of his business and his firm, with his product. You should be able to show what you can do to help this company get its work done, solve its problems or get a better share of the market.

A job interview is like an actor auditioning. The producer and the casting director have been looking for two weeks for just the right person for this part. Maybe this is the one! They want to find the right actor.

The personnel man at a large company is in the same fix. He has an opening he has to fill. Make his job easier by showing that you're the one for the job.

The first rule on job interviews is to relax and be yourself. You're qualified or you wouldn't get the interview. Dress appropriately. Then walk into the man's office, smile and introduce yourself. That's a good start.

You want to use the same techniques you learned when meeting anyone new. Stand or sit with a friendly, open stance, make eye contact, say hello, and by then the interviewer will usually take over with questions of his own. He's busy, he's seen seven women and two men for the job and he's late for his "do lunch" date with that new secretary in purchasing.

Make it easy for him. Earlier I talked about knowing something about the company. By all means research the firm, know what it does, who the big bosses are, where it is in the industry, what it's angling at on new products and tracks. Know as much about the firm as possible.

Then when you ask questions of the interviewer, make them pointed and intelligent ones. Make your questions reflect what you know about the company and its plans.

Generally don't talk too much. Ask intelligent questions. Respond to his questions briefly and to the point. Don't waste the man or woman's time. Be bright, cheerful, upbeat. Make eye contact and use an open posture. Sit up straight, don't slouch. Try sitting on the edge of the chair and see if that helps.

Be extremely careful in your use of language. Never make

any kind of racial, ethnic or sexist slurs. If you sometimes use four letter words, don't do it during an interview. Most personnel people will deduct big points from you if you swear or use foul language. Some will simply red slash your file and not under any conditions hire you. Their thinking may be: If he or she is that crude in here, how would he be out in the workplace? He could embarrass some of our more sensitive contacts and clients. We can't risk hiring him.

One last suggestion. If the person's office is new to you, look around it when you have a few seconds. If you see any signs of a hobby or activity, such as sailing, skiing or other activities mention it if you have any experience in the sport. This could be a mutual activity that would add another point to your score card.

Always leave when you sense the interview is over. The interviewer may re-arrange papers on his desk, look at the clock, or not make eye contact.

Ask: "If there's nothing more, Mr. Prokosh, I'll leave so you can get on with your other work."

Most interviews talked to liked this exit line. It showed that the applicant was observant of what was going on, and courteous enough to leave when the interview was over without any urging.

Final tip on a job interview: Enjoy it, make it fun not a chore. If you can enjoy an interview, it will come through to the person across the desk and leave him with a positive feeling about you.

ASKING FOR A RAISE:

Just mention this idea to most people in business and they suddenly get the jitters, have to go to the bathroom, get a headache, think they might throw up and then jet out of the place pleading a visit to their great aunt in the hospital.

Asking for a raise simply must be taken out of the emotional arena and looked upon as strictly a business proposition. You have something to sell, your business services. Your boss has been buying it for some time now. Since your last raise you've advanced, taken on more jobs, become more efficient. It's time to lay it out to your boss who has a lot of people to take care of and might not have followed your development.

Get ready before you do anything else. Write down these facts and memorize them.

• How long since your last raise.

• You passed your annual reviews with excellent ratings by your supervisor.

• You have moved up the responsibility chain two steps since your last raise.

• You have instigated and put into practice several new methods for getting things done in the firm which have resulted in substantial cash savings.

• If there is an opening that pays more and you're qualified, ask if you can move into that slot with the additional pay.

Now, you're ready. What you don't want to do is whine or plead. Management hates this. Don't point out that you have double the expenses now since your wife quit work and your son is in college. This is not important to the business, except that if you go broke you'll have to quit and it will develop a problem for them to replace you.

One more thing to check. How is your company doing? Is the firm making money? Is it farther ahead now than it was last year? Are the top executives getting bonuses? If you find that the company is on hard times and that the top executives have taken a cut in pay, you might postpone your plea for a raise.

The first thing you do is talk to your boss or his secretary and ask for an appointment. Make it at his convenience, not

not yours. Then arrive on time, be dressed properly for your position and smile, say hi and shake his hand if he offers it.

You're on your way, now do everything right, and we'll get together for a dinner to celebrate your raise.

OFFICE GOSSIP:

The best way to deal with office gossip is as with this type of sly invective anywhere, simply refuse to listen to it and never pass it along. Gossip can be so destructive that I've seen good workers fired for starting rumors about others in an office.

It's justified. Gossip about a person can upset the target so much that he or she can't function in the job. This causes a loss to the company and it could ruin a promising career.

If office gossip gets brutal and destructive, you have a duty to stand up for the person and put down the gossip. Only in this way can you keep the gossip mongers from launching more of their invective.

Often such rumors are started by a jilted lover or by someone who misinterprets what others do or say. In the last instance a face to face meeting can often work out the misunderstanding and get things back on the right course again.

RESPONSIBILITIES OF THE BOSS:

The lead man, the supervisor, the manager, the boss all have responsibilities too when it comes to talking with their employees.

People are people. It doesn't matter if he's the president or a new entry level clerk, everyone has feelings. It's important for the executives in a company to treat everyone with as much respect and appreciation as the boss wants to receive. A short time ago the big boss might have been only a manager somewhere. He should remember.

There are no "little people" out there. Everyone has a heart just as big as the next person, and feelings and hopes and dreams.

I've seen it a dozen times. If the boss in an office is upbeat and happy, enthusiastic and caring, generally the people in the office will be the same. Workers tend to reflect their management's temperament and ideals. Keeping a "happy ship" isn't that hard if it comes down from the top.

If the boss must discharge someone from his employment, it's usually a hard situation for both parties. Since it is so traumatic, any firing should be done in private. The boss should make every attempt to explain why the dismissal is happening, and to wish the person good fortune with another firm. Perhaps something the boss says will spark some changes in the man he had to let go.

Often a person fired needs to be asked to clean out his desk at once, to turn in his key to the front door and be escorted off the site by security.

We remember too many stories of a disgruntled former employee who returned to a company with a firearm and sprayed bullets around at all "Of the people who hurt me and were against me."

By letting an employee go with as little fuss and disruption of the daily business, you help keep the rest of the people working at the jobs they are supposed to do.

SIX RULES FOR
BETTER BUSINESS COMMUNICATION:

A president of a top firm told me some of his secrets of success. He said different methods work for different people, but these were the guidelines that he followed. They certainly had worked for him.

1. Be friendly and approachable. Say hello to the doorman, the elevator operator, the clerk, the janitor, even the vice presidents. Be free with praise when a person does a good job at any business level.

2. Be confident and work hard for what you want. Don't be afraid to ask for something if it will help the business and your own career.

3. Work hard at keeping everyone talking, keep lines of communications open with all levels of management and the work force. Nurture good relations with people across the board.

4. Be flexible. If a program fails or a plan doesn't work, shrug it off, make a note not to try that one again, and come up with a new plan to accomplish the same job. Don't hang on to a grudge, don't place blame, don't let one failure upset your whole day.

5. Work at being an excellent listener. Really hear what the other person is saying. He or she might have the answer to some problem that's been eluding you. Keep an open mind on areas of concern and don't shut out anyone.

6. Be a bulldog. Once you get your teeth into an idea or a plan, never give up because a few things go wrong. If you know the plan is good and should work, bulldog it along to the very end when it works, or it fails. No halfway measures.

So much for business, now back to the real you. Do you know who the real you is? If they asked the real you to stand up, would you realize you were supposed to jump up? If any of these questions seem ridiculous, you're probably right. So to help motivate you into improving your self image, and the real YOU, please turn to the next chapter.

18

IMPROVING YOUR
SELF IMAGE

Most of the techniques I've talked about in this book so far have been laying the groundwork for re-defining and re-directing small facets of your personality.

For example, stand in an open posture, don't cross your arms, smile and say Hi. These traits are all those of an outgoing personality, of a person who is relatively self confident, who isn't afraid of meeting new people and who is at ease meeting someone new on equal terms no matter what their title or position or what luxury car they drive.

In effect we're saying that these simple ways of being open and greeting people will help you in your daily life in all sorts of ways. If you take these suggestions to heart, you in effect will be slightly changing your personality. You will be acting in a way that's new to you, and to your surprise you'll find that the techniques work.

In this way, slowly, you will discover these new ideas are practical, that you're comfortable with them, and gradually you'll find that you are improving your own self image.

I know, dozens of books have been written on how to improve your self image, which will improve your social interrelationships, which will help your lifestyle and your business life and make you a happier, more fulfilled person.

This is not a complete course on the psychology of

personality, or of psycho-cybernetics, or of psychiatry 1206. What I want to point out is that by following many of the suggestions in this book, you will by your very actions be creating a better and more vital self image.

Take remembering names.

"Hi, I'm Charley, I heard you talking about long range fishing. Have you ever taken a seven day long range out of San Diego?"

"Charley. Hello. I'm Bryce, and I took a three day trip about a year ago."

The two of you get to comparing notes and a moment later you realize you were so interested in the fishing you forgot to use the techniques for remembering the man's name. What was it? You can't remember. So you ask him.

"Sorry, but I was enjoying our fishing talk so much I missed your name."

"I'm Bryce, rhymes with price, and I'm right, so the Bryce is right. Somebody told me once that's how they remembered my name."

"I won't forget it now, Bryce, in fact I think I've been to your canyon over in Arizona or New Mexico, once."

A year ago you wouldn't have had the guts to ask the man's name again. Now, with your new, better image of yourself, you can admit to him that you forgot his name and want to remember it. It's a simple little thing, but it's another cog in the gear that shows that you're creating a better image of yourself.

The psychologists say that if a person can change his or her self-image, they can change their personalities and their behavior.

Fine, but to me they are putting the self-image cart before the horse. Maybe you can change your self-image through utilizing some of the behavioral methods that will result in a realistic change in your personality. I still like it the other way around.

Semantics can get in the way here, I realize. But for us non professionals, what I'm trying to say is that by checking out these fifty secrets to meeting people and making friends, and by following a great number of them, you will be creating that better image and changing your meeting and greeting personality to a wonderful new degree.

SELF IMAGE PRACTICING:

Self image is how we see ourselves. I have a writer friend who is a fine fiction writer. However, he has a mind set that he can write only three hours a day. He tells me if he can get a page done an hour in his rather polished first draft, he's contented.

One day his editor called. They had just held an editorial conference and the writer's deadline for his contracted and in progress book was discussed. The book of some 500 pages was due in a month and a half. The writer was only half way through.

"I can't possibly do 250 pages in 45 days," the writer told his editor.

"It's up to you," the editor said. "My boss told me that if you didn't meet your deadline, that would automatically void your contract and you will be required to return the advance we gave you on the book."

"You're kidding," the writer said.

"Not in the least. A registered letter stating this deadline and the consequences of missing it has been sent by our legal department to you this morning. I wanted to let you know now."

The writer growled and hung up. He looked at his writing schedule. If he worked seven days a week, he had 45 days to write 250 pages. Three pages a day would be 135 pages. He couldn't do it. He wasted half a day screaming at his wife and the TV set.

Then he called his professional and selling writer friend who wrote 15 pages a day. He wanted to know how the man did it. The other writer said first he didn't write a mere three hours a day. He wrote eight to ten hours a day, running strong when the words kept flowing.

"Ten hours, don't you burn out?"

"Hell no. I get more excited as I go. When my back gives out I take an hour off for a nap."

The writer told his friend his problem.

The fast writer scoffed. "All you need to do is start working six hours a day instead of three. You write six pages a day and you'll meet your deadline."

My writer friend cursed at the idea of writing six hours a day. But there was a $20,000 advance he couldn't afford to give back. He settled down and began to convince himself he could do it.

He started and stayed at it for six hours. The first day he finished five pages. The second day he did six. The third day he did seven and the fourth day six again.

He kept a writing production chart and met his deadline on time. Now he has a new self image of his writing capability. He knows he can write more by writing longer. Now he can do ten pages a day if the deadline demands it.

EVERY DAY IN EVERY WAY:

Fads and 'isms and gurus and psycho-ridiculous plans come along every few years. In many of them there is a self examination and self criticism aspect.

One I remember asked you to sit down in a comfortable chair and close your eyes. Use soft music or silence, whichever helps you to relax.

Now all you had to do was sit there and repeat to yourself

over and over:

EVERY DAY IN EVERY WAY
I'M GETTING BETTER AND BETTER.

The amazing part is that for some people this works. The very idea that you're getting better and better at whatever you're doing gives them the mind-set so they can strive harder and move out and actually do better in their lives.

I don't knock anything that works. But for most of us, it's the lower road to a better self image. We're not about to create this super efficient individual who can step into any situation and do any job. It's easy enough to turn yourself into that personality, but the first time you slip on that super personality and jump into the breach, you'll probably find that this isn't the real you, and you can't get the job done.

Rather what we need to do in creating a better self image is to lay out in stark black and white definitions just what our honest personality and abilities are — right now. Then when we see gaps and weak points and areas we want to develop outside our present outline, we can charge ahead and accent those points. We not only find our strengths and our weaknesses, but we can expand the strengths and create that stronger, more confident, more capable individual.

We've used our imagination, our rational evaluation, and our future needs to help create a better self image. That is going to go on and transfer into personality shifts and adjustments to accommodate this new experience and new strengths that we have, which will further solidify our self image.

The two can keep on building on one another until we are reaching our own potential, and can relax and enjoy our life to its fullest.

WATCH OUT FOR FALSE BELIEFS:

"Johnny's slow, he's not nearly as smart as Phil."

What a cruel way to talk about one of your children. The worst part is that Johnny may hear that so often that he does become less than his brother Phil. Such a degrading remark can have tragic results down-life.

In grade school Johnny heard the remark often, but then as he got into junior high school and took an interest in math and science, his parents realized that he wasn't slow at all.

In high school he received straight A grades, far surpassing his brother one year ahead of him. When Johnny graduated from high school, he won a four year all expenses paid scholarship for tuition, books, dormitory and incidentals to Harvard University.

His brother joined the Air Force. Sometimes it all works out. But now is the time to look at your own false beliefs. Do you have doubts about how far you can go? Doubts about being able to learn to work a computer, to take advanced courses, to get more than a secretary's job?

Think again. Think through all of your negative implants, all of your mind sets, all of your prejudices and closed mind thinking and see if there are spots where you need to concentrate to create a better self image.

We all have them, the trick is to dig them out, let the light of logic fall on them and then smash into them with worthy effort and expect wonderful results.

Changing a self image can be the start of a great new set of experiences for you. Now is the time to take your shot!

I hope by now you know everything in this book. But, if you missed one or two, we have a shortened course, a speed read for you. Just turn the page for a quick summary of 50 SECRETS HOW TO MEET PEOPLE AND MAKE FRIENDS:

19

50 SECRETS TO MEET PEOPLE AND MAKE FRIENDS

1. STAND OR SIT WITH AN OPEN POSTURE. Don't cross your arms or legs and never hold one hand over your mouth like you don't want to talk to anyone. An open stance makes you appear more friendly and willing to talk to others. Work at this. Some men stand with arms crossed most of the time. Don't do it.

2. SMILE! Your best technique for meeting people and making friends is a wonderful smile. Use it. When you're in a new situation or don't know anyone at a party, your most important job is to smile. Show the whole world that you're friendly and approachable and would like to meet and talk. Remember, SMILE!

3. SAY HELLO OR HI: Don't be afraid to say "Hi," first. Walk up to someone who is open and smiling, smile your own best one and say "Hi, isn't this a great party?" It doesn't matter what you say, make the first move. This applies to both men and women. Be the first to say Hi and you'll find lots of people to talk to.

4. INTRODUCE YOURSELF. "I'm Charlotte, a cousin of the woman who's giving the party." Nine out of ten times the other person will respond with their name. It's the courteous thing to do, and unless the person is totally antisocial, they'll tell you their name. It's a great way to

187

get to know the names of those present.

5. REMEMBER THE PERSON'S NAME: Our names are terribly important to us. Use the remembering techniques. Repeat the person's name shortly after you hear it. "Well, Phil, I'm glad I met you because I hear you're from Kansas." Say the person's name three times. Concentrate on the name and relate it to some physical item about him or her that will trigger the name. Associations.

6. TAKE A FEW RISKS: Afraid to say Hi first? Afraid you'll be ignored or rejected? Don't be. Most people are friendly, even hunks and movie stars and gorgeous blondes. A quick rejection won't hurt you, and if you don't try, you'll always have wished you had. Maybe he's Mr. Right, and you don't even make a stab at meeting him. Won't that bug you the rest of the party?

7. ASK THOSE RITUAL QUESTIONS. It's a good way to find out about the person. "What do you do for a living?" "Do you live around here?" "Are you a friend of the hostess?" Ask those getting acquainted questions that help keep a conversation going. Keep digging until you find something you both can talk about. Be prepared to answer ritual questions about yourself as well.

8. SHOW YOUR SENSE OF HUMOR: No one likes a down in the mouth. Be ready to laugh at the other person's joke. Offer something of your own if the conversation turns to funny stories. Show that you appreciate a good joke and that you have a well developed sense of humor. Of course, don't overdo it.

9. KEEP AN OPEN MIND. One of the reasons to go to parties and meetings is to gather new information and new ideas. Keep an open mind and be ready to accept ideas and concepts even if they don't jibe exactly with your own. This is a give and take situation so be sure that you have some new ideas or comments on the subject at hand.

10. FORGETFUL? ASK AGAIN. If you forget the name

of the person you're talking to, don't be afraid to ask again. "I was so interested in what we were talking about I completely forgot your name. I won't do that again." If someone forgets your name, give it quickly with no hesitation or reluctance. Then swear to yourself that you will always remember names after this.

11. LISTEN TO WHAT THE OTHER IS SAYING: Concentrate on listening to what the other person is saying. Listen and react and show some enthusiasm for the topic. If you enjoy the subject, contribute to the discussion. If you aren't interested, attempt to change the subject to something that you both might find more challenging.

12. GIVE FREE INFORMATION. Even if the other person doesn't inquire, find a place to tell about some interesting event in your life. It's a way to keep a conversation going and to probe, to find from the other person something in his life that might be of mutual interest. The more talk the better at this first meeting stage. But, don't monopolize the conversation.

13. SIT TALL, LEAN FORWARD. In a sitting down situation, try not to slouch. It's best if you sit as tall as you can and lean slightly forward as you talk to someone. The position alone gives the others the idea that you're hanging on every word, and that you're interested in what they have to say. It works.

14. SHAKING HANDS. The good old handshake is still the best American way of greeting. Women can offer to shake hands first. Some do this to prevent the "hello kiss". Some women prefer to wait for the man to offer to shake hands. The "hello kiss" is proper if it is the accepted hello in certain societies. The Hollywood crowd all do it. Take your choice.

15. EYE CONTACT. When meeting someone for the first time, smile, then make eye contact and watch them all the way to your cheery hello and your outstretched hand.

You'll have him in the palm of your hand in five minutes. Eye contact is also vital to continue a conversation and to show your interest in what the person is saying. Use it, it works.

16. THE OPEN ENDED QUESTION. To continue a conversation, you need to ask the open ended question. This is one that can't be answered in one or two words. It usually uses words such as "how", "why", "in what way." They are questions that require a longer answer. "Just how did you get involved with the Secret Service, anyway?" That's going to take a five minute answer.

17. KNOW HOW TO LEAVE. Say you've been talking for ten minutes but you and this cute little red head have nothing in common. You can't even talk about things of mutual interest. So, look around the room, then say something like: "Well, I guess I should see our hostess before she vanishes again. Would you excuse me?" She nods, and you get up and leave and search for a new friend.

18. BRING YOUR OWN PR PERSON. The best way to get a great introduction is to bring along a friend to introduce you to those you want to meet. He might say: "Joe, you've got to meet Mandy here. She's in our sales department and she just took the west coast division sales leadership. We can't stop her. She's got vice president written all over her."

19. NAME REMEMBERING HELPS: Clear your mind of everything but the name of the person you're meeting. Repeat it silently three times. Then use it in your greeting to them. Don't think of something bright and witty to say. Remember the name first. Use some thought association. Frances is her name, she's Frail. Frail Francis. That could do it. Concentrate when introduced.

20. RE-INTRODUCING YOURSELF: Someone you met five minutes ago comes into your group and he can't remember your name. You'll see panic smash into his face. Take pity

on him. "Hi, I'm Josephine Taylor, good to meet you again. You still have those Cocker Spaniel puppies?" Take the heat off the other person and they will love you for it.

21. THE BRIEF BIOGRAPHY GREETING: "Hi, I'm Chris Larabee. I work at Fletcher Inc. and I love horses, hate football, spend half my salary on clothes and the rest buying golden oldie records of the forties and fifties." Hey, she has three feet in your conversational door before you can open your yap. What a great way to meet someone. Chris is on my Christmas card list.

22. TRY A CONVERSATION PIECE. Try carrying something that will spark conversation. A copy of "THE SUICIDE BOOK" is one that will get almost anyone over twenty talking. It's controversial, it will catch the eye and get you talking with almost anyone. Think of other conversational items you can carry to help strike up a talk with strangers.

23. MEET NEW PEOPLE: Make a little effort to meet new people. Go out of your way to greet newcomers to the neighborhood, welcome new employees to your firm or business. Invite new neighbors over for coffee and snacks, or have them come to a get acquainted party of the neighbors at your house. Be open and friendly standing in line at the post office or the grocery store. We have some new friends we see every Thursday morning when we go shopping. We call ourselves the Thursday People.

24. FACIAL AND BODY LANGUAGE: Be aware of both of these as you get into a conversation, not just at the start. Keep smiling, keep making eye contact, don't cross your arms defensively, or cover your mouth with your hand. Keep an open posture, lean forward slightly, smile and let the other person know that you're enjoying your talk.

25. IF YOU DON'T MIND TELLING ME: If you ask a personal question you think might be sensitive, always precede it with: "If you don't mind telling me..." or "I'd

love to know..." or "If it's not too personal would you tell me..." This is a casual and friendly way of saying you're interested in the other person and want to know more about them. Most people will respond favorably.

26. USE YOUR SURROUNDINGS: One good way to keep a conversation going is to use what's around you. Talk about where you are, whether it's a home, a ballroom, a fancy hotel, even a golf course or tennis court. In a home you might ask if the other person has known the host for long and how they met. Lots of items in a lovely home can be topics for conversation.

27. BE YOUR NATURAL SELF: Above all else, try to be your own natural self. Don't pretend to be someone you're not. Most of us aren't good enough actors to bring that off. Let the other person see who you are by your conversation, your selection of subjects, your reaction to his or her talk, and with your great smile and open, friendly body language.

28. PACKAGE YOUR OWN BIO: Be able to tell others who you are and what you do in a neat, concise package. "Hi, I'm John Carmen and I teach geology at San Diego state. My wife and our three kids live in the San Carlos section and we raise Cocker Spaniel show dogs." Hey, there are half a dozen items for an alert person to pick up on to keep a conversation going.

29. BE A HELLO PERSON: Make it a habit to smile and greet those you know by name. Try it. If they don't use your name in return it's probably because they have forgotten it. After a week of greeting them by name you'll probably find them return your Hi with a hello of their own and with your name. It's catching. If you're in an office, learn everyone's name, and use them.

30. NEVER REPEAT RUMORS: Gossip and rumors are the easiest way to keep a lagging conversation going, but don't fall into the trap. Once someone starts to gossip, the

conversation degenerates after that. If you run out of something to say, make a polite departure. Smile, call the person by name and say you're sure you'll see them again.

31. FIND OUT A PERSON'S BIG DREAM: Most of us have some one thing we dream of doing, some plan we want to carry out. This becomes an ideal means of continuing a conversation. Find out the dream and let the other person talk about it. You might do this by saying you always wanted to be an art student in Paris. Then ask the other person what his or her big dream is. This really works.

32. KEEP WELL INFORMED: If you go to a lot of parties, lunches and open meetings, you owe it to yourself to stay well informed. Read at least one newspaper a day, go through it page by page and read interesting stories. Listen to the news on TV and radio. Now you'll be ready to comment when someone asks you about the uprising in Tibet, or the new drop in the Federal Reserve interest rate. Keep intelligently informed.

33. EXCHANGE PERSONAL INFORMATION: One basis for making new friends is how well your interests and likes and dislikes match. You can find this out with information exchanges during a conversation. Those first few minutes will bring up information about yourself that you usually don't tell your best friends. Exchanging personal information is the best way to see if you want this person as a friend.

34. LEARN NEVER TO INTERRUPT: The best way to kill a conversation is to have one person constantly interrupting the other one. This is one of the biggest mistakes made in polite conversation. Often people do it without thinking, and without knowing that they are doing it. If your contribution is so important, wait for the right time to say it. Be polite, let the other person have his or her say.

35. BE ENTHUSIASTIC: Enjoy your conversation with

others. If you don't, move on. Be sincerely enthusiastic. A phoney will shine through a block away. Show your enthusiasm by keeping eye contact, by sitting up straight and leaning forward, and staying alert as you really listen to what the other person is saying.

36. FIND COMMON INTERESTS: The best way to develop a new friend is to find someone with common interests or goals. If you both like dogs, or stamp collecting or quilt making, you will have an immediate bond that could develop into a lasting friendship. Find these common interests by discussing your own favorite topics, hobbies and activities, and get the other person to do the same.

37. HOW TO HANDLE A TEASE: Teasing by adults is often the only way a shy person can communicate. Help them out, react, laugh and introduce yourself and get them talking. Most teasing is in fun. If it becomes destructive, speak up and call an end to it, or escort the teaser right out the front door.

38. HOW TO GIVE AN INVITATION: Always be specific about the event, set a definite time and at a stated place. This gives the person you're asking all the information. If one of the three elements won't work, you can adjust it. Say the lunch is fine and the place is right, but she gets off for her lunch from one to two instead of twelve to one. So adjust the time to one o'clock. Always be specific. Always hope for the best.

39. HOW TO MAKE A FRIEND: Be childlike. A new neighbor moves in and the kids on the block are friends with the new kids before the parents get the truck unloaded. Be open, gracious, make eye contact, say Hi first, and use your best smile. Almost all of these 50 tips will help you to make a friend.

40. DEFUSING YOUR ANXIETY: Nervous, anxious about a meeting or party? Don't be. These are regular human beings there, just like you. Be yourself, be honest. Take

a few deep breaths before you open the door and smile when you go in. Remember that most of the people in the room feel much the way you do. So smile, be first to say hello, make eye contact and be yourself. You'll do fine.

41. DEALING WITH RACIAL, SEXUAL SLURS: The best way is to speak up at once. "John, you didn't really mean what you said. That was in terrible taste." This will often bring an apology and the person will drift to a new group. The best way to deal with racial, ethnic and sexual slurs is to confront the person at once and don't let it build. Others will thank you.

42. WOMAN/MAN TALK: Men and women are interested in different things. In a conversation, try to find out what the other person is interested in and talk about that. Men talk more about activities: sports, trips, deals, adventures. Women talk more about people and their interaction. Strike a happy balance and try to get interested in the other person's favorite topic.

43. DEALING WITH CRITICISM: Constructive criticism can help, but must be given with tact, understanding, and caution. Best way: soften the blow. Say: "Phil, may I make a suggestion?" Or, "I've thought about this, and I don't want to offend you. But we're good enough friends that I can tell you." Harping and nagging will never do the job. Be cautious, constructive and make a softening statement before the criticism.

44. TALKING TO YOUR BOSS: Most good conversation tips apply, but remember he is your boss, to an extent he controls your life. Don't automatically be angry just because he's your boss. Make an appointment to see him. Be on time, state your problem or plan quickly, plainly. Leave at once when your time is up or he indicates the interview is over.

45. JOB INTERVIEW BLUES? This is your chance to solve the interviewer's problem and fill the position. Relax

and be yourself. Be on time, walk in and smile and introduce yourself. Use the same techniques when meeting anyone new. Make eye contact, keep an open posture, be alert. Know something about the company and the position if possible. Show him that you can help his company by filling the position. Leave promptly when the talk is over.

46. IMPROVE YOUR SELF IMAGE: Positive thinking about yourself helps. The hundred ways we've touched on in this book about how to converse and win friends, all speak to this same point. By being open and smiling and saying Hi first and making eye contact, you'll be doing things to slightly alter your own personality. This will help your self image. Knock out negative thinking and false beliefs. Concentrate on being better and better every day. Just thinking that way helps make it work.

47. HOW TO GET A DATE: Follow the steps in meeting/greeting/making friends. You'll find dates in these parties and meetings. Concentrate on going to meetings that involve your favorite hobby or activity. Meet other enthusiasts about gardening at a garden club. Join a hiking group if you like to hike. Join a writer's group if you write. Join singles groups. Work at it but in a logical, intelligent way. You'll get results.

48. LEARN TO FLIRT: Flirting has been described as being aggressively and uninhibitedly friendly. Flirting has a bad name but it is done more in the name of fun than anything. Flirting is eye contact with a hunk or knockout across a room. It's returning a stare for a stare, a grin, a smile. Avoid the pick up lines. Be honest and fun. Learn how to flirt and how not to go farther than you want to go.

49. ENDING A CONVERSATION: If you're sitting down, stand, it's a sure signal that the talking is over. Look around the room. Check your watch. Summarize what you've been talking about. Then say something like: "George, it's been fun talking to you, but now I have to meet with the

hostess about some of the arrangements. You circulate now and meet lots of new people."

50. BASIC INSTRUCTIONS: Always start and end a conversation with eye contact, use the person's name and a warm handshake. Keep it all pleasant. Someone you meet today might be your boss tomorrow, or be ready for a big order, or need a fourth for bridge, or a new writer on a broadway play that's in trouble and needs a rewrite. Most important: Enjoy talking with and meeting new people and making friends. Friends are the most important element in the lives of most of us.